International Bicycle Touring

From the Editors of
Bike World Magazine

$2.95

WORLD PUBLICATIONS
P.O. BOX 366
MOUNTAIN VIEW, CA. 94040

P9-DTL-933

CONTENTS

COVER DESIGN BY JEFF LOUGHRIDGE

INTRODUCTION

If you want to know *everything* about bike touring in foreign countries, this is probably the wrong book. If you're after total predictability and security, why not use more comfortable transportation and stay at the big American hotels instead of plodding along on your bike?

Obviously, you'll miss something that way. It's not just quaintness and charm, sunshine and the great outdoors that you're after when you decide to take a bike tour of France. It's the unexpected that makes the great stories you can tell your friends for years.

You could program your way through Europe or other parts of the world in such a way that nothing will ever happen. You can play the role of an international traveller, getting a taste of jet-set living without the expense and confirming reservations through hotel clerks and maitre d's.

You could have written the whole plot without leaving Peoria, except perhaps for the excitement of failing to find a cab in Paris and almost missing your plane as a result, or learning to your disappointment that peanut butter is impossible to find in Hamburg.

Many confirmed bike travellers are still tied to their own conceptions of how to tour. They want to know in advance exactly what to expect. But there's a point beyond which factual information becomes more burdensome than useful. Certainly you want to have good maps showing the road gradients; you want to know about accommodations, the availability of bicycle parts, access to goods and services and so on. But that's only the necessary foundation of bicycle touring. Cycling in foreign countries should be 90% inspirational and only 10% perspiration and worry. To be constantly buried in your maps and guidebooks while passing through Europe is lamentable.

We've emphasized a very strong framework for bike touring in this book, on which you can build your own experience. Three things can prevent problems from ruining your trip: good equipment, know-how and the right attitude. The articles in *International Bicycle Touring* were written by cyclists who've been riding long enough to iron out the difficulties that often get in the way of having a good time.

James Brooks has travelled extensively in Europe by bicycle. He has written excellent no-nonsense articles on packing a bike for the airlines, riding with a spouse and crossing international borders.

Jim McNeeley, a state congressman from West Virginia, is a contributor to *Bike World* magazine. His down-to-earth article on road hazards comes from personal experience—he's the one who hit the chicken.

Lloyd Sumner is a living legend, for his around-the-world tour that ended in late 1975, for his topnotch expertise in travelling light and inexpensively, and for his "together" cycling philosophy. When he is home working, Lloyd is an internationally-known designer of computer art.

Clifford Graves, a San Diego physician, is the president of the International Bicycle Touring Society. There is probably no more than a handful of avid touring cyclists in this country who aren't familiar with Dr. Graves and his organization. He is also widely known and respected in European cycle touring circles; he was a personal friend of cardiologist Dr. Paul Dudley White, and is a frequent contributor to *Bike World.*

1

AN EYE ON THE WORLD

In this chapter, we cover the basics, the practical things that, along with common sense, you'll need wherever you go: what kind of bike to use, what to take along and how, dangers to avoid and orienting your thinking. Not only husbands and wives, but anyone planning to travel with a friend, should read the section on "Learning to Compromise." An argument over which route to take the next day can be twice as destructive 3000 miles away from home. A new way to look at your needs and your relations with people and nature is introduced in "Passport to Freedom," proving that touring by bicycle can be as mind-expanding as any occult experience.

For the First Timer

People who have been cycling a long time make an emphatic distinction between what they call the "cyclist" and the "bicyclist" or "bicycle rider." This section is for the "bicycle rider" — the person who may not have owned a bicycle since childhood.

Many people have very fuzzy ideas about what it's like to buy, ride and maintain a bicycle. The bicycle is such a 'nice' machine, with such a sweet public relations image that most beginners assume it'll never turn and bite them. They pay too much for a machine that doesn't fit them with components that can't be serviced or replaced in the countries where they'll be traveling.

They don't know the first thing about bicycle maintenance and get stuck in the remote moors of Scotland with broken spokes, chains, cables, derailleurs, lost cotter pins and crank bolts, loose pedals, and so on. They ride off on saddles of sadistic design on rigid schedules of "easy" 50-mile days, on the advice of friends who cycle over 100 miles a week at home. You can imagine the results.

Buying a Bicycle For Touring

Many 10-speed bikes in the $150-$200 price range are suitable for long tours while carrying baggage. Motobecane's Grand Touring, at the high end of this range, is notable for its excellent choice of components throughout. Raleigh, Peugeot, Gitane and other big names make very serviceable models.

The pitfalls of choosing· a bike are too numerous to mention: short-distance racing bikes that shake your teeth out when ridden all day, hidden flaws in hand-built frames, essential and costly derailleur and wheel changes, frames without eyelets for mounting fenders and racks, etc.

Before paying for your bike, insist that it be set up with a bottom gear in the low-30-inch range. The Shimano Crane GS, Shimano 600 and Sun Tour VGT are the best touring derailleurs available; Simplexes are also serviceable.

The most important single factor is that the bicycle be comfortable to ride for hours at a time. Make absolutely certain the bike "fits" you. You should be able to straddle the top tube with both feet flat on the ground, with about ½"-1" of clearance. Have the shop attendant set the saddle and bars at proper height before your test ride. Before buying, ride many different bikes. You'll find that some seem "right" for you, due to a mix of saddle height, top tube length, handlebar style, wheel base, bottom bracket height and frame angles that closely conforms to your specific body dimensions.

Make your test rides long — several miles at least. Don't buy right away — go home and reflect deeply: were there nagging little sensations that you wanted to dismiss, but which might become unbearable after a week on the road?

You may find the bent-over drop-handlebar riding position awkward at first, but you'll get used to it. Even professional racing cyclists do most of their riding with their hands "on the tops" so don't feel you'll look like a dude unless you ride "on the drops" all the time. Drop handlebars put the body in the most efficient position for delivering power to the cranks and for a streamlined profile.

Several new bikes in the price range previously mentioned have absolutely rotten saddles. If yours comes with a plastic-framed seat with the cover carelessly stapled on, exchange it immediately. A good saddle is, unfortunately, expensive. Top of the line are the Ideale 90 IR, which is factory-softened but which will stain all but black riding shorts for several months; the Cinelli padded, leather-covered models with nylon frames;

and "The Seat," a comfort-designed product that soothes most, but not all, posteriors.

Test ride a saddle before you buy as men and women have different requirements for riding comfort and some of the top-liners don't fit everyone. Expect to pay $25-$30 for an extremely long-lasting, comfortable saddle.

During your test ride, sit up and ride no-hands on a windless, flat surface. Does the bike track straight ahead? If not, the frame may be misaligned — don't buy it or you may have serious handling or chainline problems. Ride on a rough surface and see whether the bike handles and absorbs shock well. Take a fast downhill spin and check for shimmy in the front end. It may only be a loose headset. Stop and lift the front end, bouncing the front tire lightly on the ground. If the handlebar-to-fork assembly wiggles in the head tube, ask the dealer to tighten it, then go out and try the hill again.

Signs that the bike isn't "made for you" are: a feeling that you're leaning too far forward to reach the top of the bars. This can be remedied by replacing the handlebar stem with a shorter one, or may mean the top tube is just too long — but beware: too short a stem deteriorates handling stability; a feeling that you're in an inefficient position over the pedals (usually too far forward — may be remedied by moving the saddle forward or back, or may mean that the frame is designed for a person with shorter or longer legs, or is just plain poorly designed); a feeling that the bike is either too "nervous" or "sluggish" (may be due to frame design, frame tube steel, etc.).

If you haven't ridden since childhood, many 10-speed bikes may feel "nervous" to you; too-steep frame angles and too-short fork rake are indicated if the bike tends to oversteer (when you turn just a little and get a much greater, faster change in direction than you intended). A certain amount of responsiveness is preferable to the "dead" feel of cheap bike frames, but there are bikes whose nervy qualities will be dangerous when you're fully loaded, or which will give you the sensation of having spent the day working with a jackhammer. Adult 10-speed bikes sold in the US come with 27 by 1¼" wheels. These are not available on the Continent, so have the dealer fit your machine with the European 700C tire size. Don't try 26" or 650C wheels on a frame intended for the 27" size.

Buy a name-brand bike in the $150-$200 new-price range, with wide-range gearing and a good saddle. Either have the dealer mount toe clips and straps and get used to riding with them, or take a set home and mount them after you feel secure on the bike. Straps should be loose enough to enable your foot to slide in and out easily, but tight enough and of the proper size to keep the ball of your foot centered over the pedal axis.

Cycling shorts with *chamois* linings are worth their price in comfort. They should be washed frequently to prevent accumulation of bacteria which can contribute to painful saddle sores.

Cycling gloves are a blessing, should you fall and come down on your hands. They also help prevent numb hands resulting from compression of the ulnar nerve in the palm. Get the French type with really good padding stitched in a spiral pattern into the palms.

Racks and Bags

Once you have left the bike shop and have tested your cycle for a couple of weeks, you might want to think about load carrying gear.

Starting from the bike up, the best luggage racks are sold by the Touring Cyclist Shop, Box 4009, Boulder, CO 80302. You might as well consider panniers. They are cyclist-designed and, although expensive, the best around. Avanti's bags are also bikie-designed and an excellent value.

The best handlebar bag in terms of features and durability is the Touring Cyclist Shop's TA-LaFuma model, a big, square, practical French model with a very usable map pocket on top and small-gear pockets on the front. The Touring Cyclist Shop will send their catalog free upon request.

Under the general heading of accessories — you shouldn't cycle at night, but be prepared in case you have to — the perfect bicycle light has not been designed yet. *Bike World* magazine's medical editor, Craig Hoyt, MD, raced in France's infamous 750-mile Paris-Brest-Paris marathon. (He finished in just over 60 hours.) Hoyt took the most popular cycling light along and found to his chagrin that the batteries quickly went dead and the lamp just didn't give enough illumination for safe, fast night riding. All the French veterans were using multi-cell flashlights taped to their handlebar stem.

Speedometers, odometers, bike flags, horns and kickstands are dead weight for the long-distance tourer. Take a good lock and chain or cable and don't leave your bike or your bags unattended. Take your bags off and bring them inside when you stop for food, or have a riding partner stay outside with them.

Dressing for the Weather

Some cyclists won't use fenders come hell or high water. If you're among their hardened ranks, fine. Others should be aware that most of Europe and Asia get hit with summer rain. On a 21-day early-summer tour through Germany, France, Italy and Switzerland, it rained 18 days. Ride in the morning and you'll miss most of the rain; it's not as bad in late summer anyway, and the Mediterranean countries are relatively rain-free in summer.

The light plastic *Bluemels* fenders are probably the best solution. Have them mounted with lock washers and check tightness every evening during your trip.

The best rain protection is the Bellwether cycling cape, which has thumb loops to keep the front from blowing around, a body strap to keep it from blowing up in back and a protected air vent to prevent condensation in the shoulder area.

The cape comes with spats to keep most of the rain off your lower legs.

You may not ever have spent as much time outdoors as you will during your trip. Sunburn can bum you out for many days. Protect your nose, lips, face, arms and legs. Be extremely conservative in this regard. Take sunglasses and a cap with a visor.

If you're riding in cycling shorts, put on extra-thick layers of suntan lotion and repeat at frequent intervals during the day.

The body adapts slowly, over a period of days, to hot weather exercise. During the adaptation period you'll also be putting demands on your stress-adaptation mechanisms. This makes you a prime candidate for illness. Until you feel fit and strong, eat carefully and keep your distances short.

The exercising body is fueled by natural sugars, minerals and enzymes. This means, eat lots of fresh fruit and vegetables. The rested, not-overtaxed, body is incomparably more resistant to disease. So get in shape before you leave.

Camping Gear

Unhappiness is sleeping in a two-pound down mummy bag on a warm midsummer night. Average seasonal temperature ranges for Europe can be found in the Hawkins' book *Bicycle Touring in Europe*. Keep in mind whether you're a "cold sleeper" or not, whether you wear a lot of clothes to bed and whether you carry a tent. For a thorough, tested guide to bicycle camping, get Raymond Bridge's excellent *Freewheeling: The Bicycle Camping Book*. For summer use in places where rain is likely, the most versatile bag lining is one of the recent synthetics.

A seldom heard suggestion is to take a moderate-to-warm-weather bag and also pack along a near-weightless pair of down booties. When cold weather sets in, your feet stay warm.

Well-designed bags and panniers are essential for a comfortable tour. (Ted Mock)

While researching our book *Travelling by Bike*, we made a long careful study of tent quality and efficiency factors. Here, in the most general terms, are the results.

Modern nylon lightweight tents are expensive. Any water-proofed single-walled tent will produce unbearable condensation and drip inside during wet or dry weather. The common solution is a porous nylon inner tent with a waterproof "fly" pitched over it. A well-made, inexpensive, cotton tent, with a relatively lightweight waterproof nylon fly bought separately to be pitched over it, or erected alone for minimal shelter in hot-weather conditions, is also recommended.

If you've got the money to stay at a hotel when it rains, forget the tent. You might take the 9' by 12' light waterproof nylon tarp for shelter in dire emergencies, along with a few aluminum pegs and some light nylon rope.

Cooking and eating gear should be light and simple: aluminum pots, camper's knife, fork and spoon in a small pouch, collapsible plastic bottles, plastic bowl or dish, a cup. Campers who like to cook get along with a single pot and one heavy spoon. The pot is used as a cooking, serving and drinking utensil. The spoon will handle about anything else.

Clothing

The ever-practical Lloyd Sumner recommends one pair of pants, one pair of shorts, one shirt, one sweater, one pair of shoes, one set of underwear and three socks.

If you find you've brought too much, you can always ship unneeded clothes home.

Specialized cycling clothing is designed for utmost practicality. We've mentioned the desirability of chamois-lined pants and padded gloves already. But a cycling jersey is perhaps not optimal gear for the touring cyclist. Ordinary T-shirts, long-sleeved shirts and blouses, sweaters and windbreakers can be worn at restaurants where cycling jerseys might be inappropriate.

Cycling shoes are likewise not necessary, perhaps not even optimal, for the slow-paced tourist. They're not comfortable for long walks, which means that if you enjoy walking through strange towns in the evening or hiking side trips, you'll have to pack the extra weight of another pair of shoes.

Cameras and Photography

Competition is intense in the pocket rangefinder camera market. Consequently, the general quality is good. Canon's Canonet QL17, for about $110, is perhaps the best buy.

When boarding planes, don't take unexposed film in or out of the camera through metal detector gates. Some metal-detecting equipment can fog your film. Hand camera and film to the attendant for separate inspection.

Wherever you're going, read the best available travel guides prior to departure. Some countries in Asia allow you to take only a certain number of rolls of film into the country. Kodak films are available world-wide, but you'll save weight by buying film upon arrival.

You'll avoid return-trip hassles by registering your foreign made camera before you leave. You won't be charged duties when you bring it back into the US.

Camera stores salespeople and photography magazines make it sound as if modern automatic and semi-automatic cameras will "make" good pictures. This is not true. The quickest way to learn good basic photo composition and procedures is to take a school course on the subject. Experience is the only teacher in photography. It might make the difference between an artistic and an excruciatingly embarrassing slide show.

One area in which good advice is seldom given by camera shop clerks or photography class teachers, is in the choice of films to be used by the neophyte traveller — Kodachrome 25 is a good choice, not only because of its good color balance and fine grain, but because it has good "latitude."

Riding Skills

The most important riding skill is pacing. We've mentioned planning short distance hops for the start of your tour. There is another kind of pacing. A number of beginning cyclists often choose a very large gear for flat country travel and stick to it all day long. Laboratory research has revealed that the best endurance gear — the one you'll be able to ride in longest and fastest without fatigue — is one you can easily "spin." For most beginners, this will be a gear in the low to mid-60-inch range.

Riding position plays an important role in long-distance comfort. An experienced shop attendant can help you out with this. However, you will be the final judge, so don't be afraid to make small, tentative changes in search of ideal saddle and bar height and front-to-rear saddle position.

The beginning cyclist is often unaware of how unsafe it really is to ride a bicycle on the same road with a heavy volume of cars and trucks. The accident most beginners dread is being hit from behind. In actual fact, rear-end collisions account for less than three per cent of bike-car accidents. In most of these rare cases, the cyclist was at fault, having suddenly drifted into the automobile's path.

The real danger for the cyclist in traffic comes at intersections. The driver turning right, who doesn't see you because he's looking left for traffic, and the car backing out of a driveway are the cyclist's greatest hazards.

The way to stay alive in traffic is to be *visible* and *predictable.*

The *"be seen"* rule applies with added force at corners. When approaching corners it is especially important to ride out at the left edge of the right-turn lane.

When you're stopped at an intersection and the light turns green or a policeman waves you through, always look left for late intersection-stormers.

In light traffic you can make your left turns from the auto left-turn lane. When preparing to glide over into the left-turn lane, check behind you for traffic and give yourself plenty of distance to move in. If you're about to move left to clear a protruding car, stopped bus, etc., look back and make sure you have the oncoming driver's eye-contact. If not, let him or her pass.

It is safe and easy to ride in the motorized traffic mix. Obviously though, it's not always pleasant. Therefore it is a good reason to tour in countries that have a large network of rideable secondary roads.

Hill riding demands strong legs and low gears. Gearing changes take only a few minutes at bike shops and are not expensive. Shift down before you need to when approaching a hill; this preserves your rhythm and avoids last-minute changes while lugging down.

Don't risk your life for the thrill of a fast downhill run on an unfamiliar road. A small patch of gravel on a curve, loss of control due to a heavy load of baggage and a strange road banking can be hazardous.

Unexpected gravel should be ridden very conservatively — don't brake and don't turn. Railroad and trolley tracks, especially in the rain, should be crossed at as near a right angle as possible.

Maintenance and Repairs

The last thing people on vacation want to think about is grease and ball bearings. Consider the alternative. You're in Rothenburg in southern Germany. It's Monday and you get a flat tire. You don't know how to change it so you hunt for a bike shop. It's a Catholic holiday and nobody's working. You walk five miles before finding someone who happens to have dropped by his shop for an hour; he is utterly incredulous over the fact that you can't perform this basic five-minute repair. You feel like an oaf.

Bike repair is easy. When you take the cranks off to regrease the bottom bracket axle for instance, you don't run into anything like the inside of a 17-jewel watch. You don't

want to learn about repairs while you're out on the road. Get
Tom Cuthbertson's entertaining *Anybody's Bike Book* right
now, several months ahead of your trip, and start fooling
around with your bike. You'll get immense satisfaction out of
being able to make your own repairs. Acquire the tools you'll
need as you explore one section of your bike's anatomy at a
time.

Take along a new spare inner tube; that way you can wait
until evening to put a patch on the tube that's gone flat. It is
good practice to take spokes along with you. Also take brake
and derailleur cable spares, and brake blocks. A couple of extra
chain links and a chain breaker can also be useful.

If you insist on popping off to ride overseas without any
notion of bike maintenance, at least read Cuthbertson's book
on the plane. Cram all the tools he recommends for basic
maintenance into your pockets at the last minute. Don't forget
your crank tool. New cotterless cranks sometimes work loose
for the first 500 miles of riding or so, and you'll ruin your
cranks by riding on them while they're loose.

Where to Go

There's a California cyclist, just over 40 years old, whose ideal cycling vacation is three weeks in the Alps, during which he'll ride 2,000 miles total and climb up to 17,000 feet, over eight passes, in a single day. The mountains really inspire him.

Lloyd Sumner says the 750 miles of Australia's desolate Nullarbor Plain was one of the most rewarding segments of his around-the-world ride. Sumner is a philosopher and nature lover who appreciates solitude.

Clifford Graves' International Bicycle Touring Society groups have a good time just about everywhere they go.

No one has ever heard Bill Marquardt say there was a place, a person or a landscape he *didn't* enjoy. Marquardt's tour stories are a constant series of conversations with the natives. Marquardt on the Nullarbor Plain would be a terrible thing to happen — but he'd undoubtedly find someone to talk to even in the middle of the Outback.

It is suggested that the international cycle tourist *not* overprogram his trip. But in accordance with the principle that the only good planning prevents trouble, you *should* tour areas that are not hopelessly at odds with your own likes, dislikes, approaches to interpersonal relations and so on. Cycling does bring you close to the people, the weather, and the performance capacity of your own body. So don't plan on making yourself miserable.

Europe

An excellent reference book is Karen and Gary Hawkins' *Bicycle Touring in Europe*, available for $2.95 from World Publications, Box 366, Mt. View, CA 94040. The Hawkins book describes each European country by geography and road system, as well as accommodations, climate, and access from other countries.

It's not easy to meet people in the big European cities. It depends a lot on what kind of people you want to meet, and whether you care about meeting people at all. If you stay in youth hostels, you'll meet lots of fellow travellers of all nationalities. If you belong to any kind of religious, fraternal, cultural, occupational or political organization or society here, you might find instant friendship abroad.

Most likely you will just be "passing through," and it's a little unrealistic to expect deep, lasting friendships to form all the time, yet there's a brief, but heart-warming feeling that you'll find everywhere; maybe it's from a cop who wants to make very sure you understand the way to the *Jugendherberge*, or the Italian grocery clerk and her 12-year-old daughter who have all the time in the world to laugh at your sign language. Possibly the Swiss youth hostel warden who "doesn't have much for dinner," then sets the table with garden-fresh salad and strawberries and a gigantic platter of spaghetti.

It's silly to plan to cycle across the Alps from Germany to Italy if you haven't ridden a bike since you spun hookers on your Rollfast. Believe *nothing* that anyone tells you about daily mileage if you're not an experienced cyclist. To start, choose a place like England or France, where the country towns are very close together and the roads lightly travelled, and forget about miles. It might even be better to buy your bike six months ahead of the trip and work out the bugs close to home.

Clifford Graves' suggested tours and tips on cycling in specific countries of Europe will help a lot. There isn't a single Western European country where you *can't* have a good time, depending on what you expect and how you relate to the riding and cultural conditions.

Asia

Unless you plan to do a lot of hopping around on boats

and planes or explore one area heavily, we don't recommend a cycling tour to Asia for the first-timer. Island-hopping by plane and strict customs procedures at nearly all borders demand patience and expertise. Asian customs and languages are radically different from ours; they require that you make a thorough study of appropriate literature before you go.

If you're an experienced cycle tourist, who has already criss-crossed Europe or has a special interest in the Orient, places such as Japan, Taiwan, New Zealand, Australia and India may be of interest. As you will discover from Lloyd Sumner's article, Indonesia is not for beginners. Cycling in Nepal, to be pleasant, takes willingness to quarter with families, often sleeping with the goats and chickens. In order to appreciate Nepal's Himalayan wonders, you should also be willing to leave the bike and go hiking for several days at a time.

Learning to Compromise

by James Brooks

I've never traveled abroad without my wife. When I think of some of the situations and places I've landed in while hitch-hiking around the United States before we were married, I'm glad that our European travels have had the benefit of her restraining influence.

Last summer one of our European tour group leaders from DeKalb Bike Club had two weeks free and took off alone for the Alps, looking forward to riding at his own speed. Although he is fluent in five European languages, he was back within three days with a bad case of the lonelies. "It was so beautiful and there was no one there to share it with," he complained.

It's the aspect of shared experience that really differentiates overseas travel from home riding. At home I ride either for training or just to be out feeling good. In either case I prefer to ride alone, giving my thoughts and fantasies free rein. But once overseas the scenery becomes more interesting than the familiar corn and bean fields of DeKalb County.

My wife and I present the classic confrontation: she rides comfortably at about eight m.p.h. and likes to take a break about once an hour. To me an easy touring pace is 16-18 m.p.h. with a short break every 30 miles or so. When I'm getting out of the saddle to stand and attack a hill, Lynne is getting out of the saddle to walk up it. Somehow we have to learn to ride together well in advance of a trip overseas. After all, a trip is a vacation. A couple gets to enjoy each other's company more thoroughly on vacation than time will allow during the rest of the year. Certainly it's better to be in a loving mood after a day of traveling.

Bill Vetter

Well in advance of the trip, agree on a day that is going to
be your day to ride together. About this time the man must
assume a fairer share of the household duties. Continuing to
carry out the garbage and mow the lawn isn't enough. If he
doesn't pitch in with vacuuming, dusting, laundry, and other
time-eating chores, she doesn't have time to take a full day off
every week for bicycling.

The next step is equal equipment. If an inequity must exist
it should favor the weaker rider. Ask yourself, was your pro
bike bought at your wife's expense? Ride together on equal
bikes instead of relegating her to Aunt Harriet's used 3-speed.
I'd recommend that you look for touring bikes at your local
bike shop in the $200 range and weighing 25-28 pounds. I do
not mean that they should necessarily be the same frame size or
even the same color. But they should have the same type of
frame, derailleurs, crank set, brakes, and other components.
Thus one tool set fixes both. They should have quick release
hubs and I'd recommend that you get them mounted with
Bluemel plastic fenders if traveling to Northern Europe or the

British Isles. While we're at the old bike shop, take a long look at cycling shorts (2-3 pair each) with chamois crotch, a couple of jerseys each, and gloves.

Cycling shoes with cleats are usually too much of a hassle for overseas touring. You'll do a great deal more walking there than you would think at first. Walking on cycling shoes is the worst treatment you can give them. You'll quickly break or erode the cleat, and you'll break down the shoe's shank, causing your unsupported heel to droop while riding. This will lead to knee problems. I prefer good quality jogging shoes. They are spongy compared to riding shoes, but they fit in the toe clips well and are heaven to walk on.

Once properly outfitted you're ready to start riding together in earnest. It is vital that the stronger rider see his role as one of giving encouragement by word rather than example. You'll find it necessary to shift to a lower gear and pedal slower if there is a significant disparity. Wear one of those rear view mirrors so you can tell if you are running away when going single file. Take the lead when riding into the wind, and, when traffic permits, take the windward side in a crosswind.

When making suggestions, weigh your words carefully. What might seem to be a helpful comment can easily be taken as an insult by someone on the verge of exhaustion. Take a sip of water at least every five miles and learn to pass the bottle back and forth without running into each other.

Rides with your local club offer great encouragement for working up to touring distances of 30-50 miles. Both of you get the same patch for participating. Once again, a tangible shared experience. But even after you have ridden a 50-60-mile club ride together you may still find an uncomfortable discrepancy in your normal speeds. Praise the accomplishment rather than pointing out how much more progress yet remains. Such encouragement should help your partner to make the effort to get out every day during the week for 10-15 miles.

Our final confidence builder is the solo ride. Pick a

destination 25-30 miles leeward. The stronger rider packs a picnic lunch and his or her bike into the car. The other partner takes a cue sheet and with only his or her bicycle and water bottle, rides the distance solo, with the wind. It should take two hours or less. After lunch he or she drives the car back and you ride into the wind. Comparing times may surprise you.

Not understanding how to make minor adjustments on a bike keeps more riders close to home than anything else. Your riding partner should learn to do everything that you can do. That includes changing and patching a tire, adjusting brakes, derailleurs, saddle position; and assembly and disassembly for shipping. Your role should be confined to that of tool hander and advisor. In most cases you will also have to teach something about tools so it will be understood why wrenches are used on bolts instead of a pair of pliers. Ditto for tire irons over screw drivers.

Before leaving we have to come to agreement on what each person feels are the most vitally important parts of the trip. Perhaps the worst argument Lynne and I ever had was over the Louvre. To me the Louvre is less an art museum than a tourist trap which exists to parade other nations' works which have been plundered by the French, the spoils of Napoleonic conquest. I wanted to spend the day exploring bike shops. Lynne had wanted to see Paris all her life, and to her Paris meant the Louvre. We went to the Louvre. A sensible person would agree before leaving on those things which are non-negotiable—which must be seen.

Certainly not every couple who travels together will be a married couple, nor will the man always be the most enthusiastic cyclist. But in any possible combination of two or more people there will be a strongest and a weakest rider. Understanding this and dealing with it in advance will mean the difference between having a traveling companion or a rolling battle.

Packing Up Your Bike

by James Brooks

There are people who feel the best way to ship your bike on an airplane is to show up at the airport with it and confound the airport personnel with your audacity.

A bike fouls up the already-hectic world of the baggage handler. First of all, it doesn't fit on the baggage conveyor. It must be lugged through a crowded airport lobby to one of those unmarked doors where it is dragged down a flight of stairs, bumpety-bump. Then it is thrown onto an open-sided truck with a ton or so of assorted luggage and disappears into the maw of the plane. Just understand that your odd-shaped, awkward, bulky bicycle makes waves for the baggage handler. He gets irritated. Even on a good day a baggage handler wouldn't know the difference between a 531 double-butted-throughout, full-Campagnolo bike and his kid's trashmo.

On the way overseas you should pack your bike so securely that it could be sent through the US Postal Service without damage. Assembly and disassembly will make you more familiar with your bike, which will give you confidence boxing and unboxing it when it comes time to leave.

But first, a word about tools. Assuming you are not going to be riding on tubular tires, go out and buy the following items: two spare inner tubes of good quality, a patch kit, a set of three tire irons, a cheap metric wrench set—eight, nine, 10 11, 12, 13, 14, 15, 17 and 19 millimeter (open-end wrenches provide the above on five wrenches; a Mafac kit does not have the big sizes you will need) and a sharp pocket knife. It's also a good idea to bring 10 spokes that fit both front and back wheels, a rear brake cable, a rear derailleur cable and a pair of spare brake blocks.

Add to the above any further tools which you know how to use. If you are riding tubulars, replace the tire irons with tubular rim cement wrapped in a plastic bag, and consider buying two spare tubulars in Europe instead of at home. Take a crank tool for cotterless cranks.

Mount all new rubber and be prepared to patch your tubes if you get a run of bad luck. Whatever you do, don't let your bike shop talk you into buying new wheels to replace your tubular tires with either 27-inch or 700C regular tires. You can't get 27-inch tires in Europe, or 7000C tires in the States when you come back.

If you buy all your touring gear from a single bike shop you will be well known there and can ask the shop owner to save you a bike carton in your frame size. Get a good one that was opened carefully and hasn't been crushed on the ends.

Also find some single-wall corrugated material to wrap your frame tubes. This is optional, but will keep the scratches to a minimum. Wrap a single thickness around the three main tubes, the fork blades and the four rear stays. Ask your dealer to show you how a new bike comes out of the box so you'll have an idea of how it's done.

Record your bike's serial number, make, model, size, and color and put this information with your passport and other papers. If your bike, camera or other equipment was made outside the United States it should be declared to customs before departure.

Now take a small piece of electrician's tape and place it on your seat post at the point where it enters the downtube. With the proper seat height marked you won't have to spend the first couple of days of your trip making constant adjustments. Mark your stem height the same way.

Loosen your seat post bolt. Chances are it will take a 13- or 14-mm wrench. If you have center-pull brakes, check to see if you can tighten the seat post nut without turning the brake cable stop. If the bolt doesn't have a flush head you can hold it in place with another wrench while tightening the nut.

Remove the seat post and saddle and set them aside as a unit. Loosen the stem bolt two complete turns. Many newer stems have recessed bolts which will take a six- or seven-mm Allen wrench. Sears makes long-arm Allen wrench sets which give you sufficient torque when it comes to tightening up again. In any case, don't loosen this bolt more than two full turns or tigers will leap out at you. (Actually, you may just drop the expander bolt — a nuisance.)

Put a piece of wood on top of the bolt and give it a sharp rap with a hammer. The entire stem and handlebar assembly will now lift out. Do not disconnect the brake cables. If you have stem shifters you will have to loosen the screw which holds them onto the stem and lift the stem free of the shifter collar. For the moment just hook the handlebars over the top tube.

If you have toe clips and straps there won't be any confusion between your right and left pedals. Is the 15-mm wrench in your metric set thin enough to fit between the pedal and the crank arm? If not, have your bike shop crack them loose for you. You can then get them off and on by using two cone wrenches at once, held together to avoid spreading the ends. Most people have a lot of difficulty figuring out which way to turn the pedals, since the left pedal has left-hand threads. On either pedal you turn the wrench toward the back of the bike to loosen, and toward the front of the bike to tighten.

If your front wheel is held on with nuts, remove it and see if you can find one of those flat plastic discs at your bike shop that can be put on the axle end to prevent it from punching a hole in the box. If you have a quick release, remove the skewer assembly entirely and put it in one of your touring bags. Don't lose the springs. Loosen the nut which holds your front brake in place and turn the brake slightly to the side. Then turn the fork around.

Now tie the front wheel to the left side of the bike frame's main triangle. Use slip knots. Next hook the handlebar through the wheel and the frame and tie it in place.

Put the bike in the box. Slip the pedals and the seat assembly down the side to the bottom and tie them to the bike. Your tire pump and *empty* water bottle should be on the bike. There will also be room down the side of the box to stuff your handlebar and seat bag at least, and possibly your panniers. Put light stuff like clothes in these bags and put heavy stuff like your camera, tools and spare parts in your carry-on bag to keep your overweight charge to a minimum. Most airlines allow you 44 pounds and will zap you approximately $2 a pound for overweight. Coming back you pay it again.

Make sure your passport, traveler's checks and other papers are not in one of the bags which you are about to seal up in the bike carton. Use filament tape to seal the carton. Do not tie it with rope or baggage handlers will pick it up by the rope and crush the carton.

Take a marking pen and write your name, address, destination, departure date, airline, and flight number on the outside of the box. At the end of the box write down the make, model, size, color, and serial number of your bike. If your bike was made outside the United States it must be declared with US Customs at the airport before you check in. It is helpful if your shipping box is for the same make of bike which you are carrying. You may be asked to open the box to show the customs man that a bike is indeed inside. For this reason the box should only be taped-up sufficiently to get your bike safely to the airport. In your carry-on luggage put the roll of filament tape that you will need to repack your bike at the airport and when you come home.

To reassemble your bike once you land, just read this article backwards.

Road Hazards Around the World

by Jim McNeely

I admit it — I'm the guy who hit the chicken. Yep, there was a burst of feathers and a taste of gravel. You see, I was cruising this Tennessee gravel road, not even thinking about road hazards. . .

There are a number of things existing on, beside, around, or as a part of a road that can do a cyclist grievous harm. Besides chickens, that is. As a cyclist leaves the busy highways generally traveled in the US and seeks the quiet by-ways of other countries or of rural areas in our own US, a multitude of hazards present themselves. It might be beneficial to take a look at several of these. Forethought might well help to keep a cyclist's tour from ending in a "taste of gravel."

Looking at Animals

The dog, in many rural parts of the world, is a kind of "sacred cow." The US Southern Appalachians, for example, have a great many valuable (and valued) dogs running loose. In general, whether it be for herding, hunting, guarding, or eating, residents of rural areas are oftentimes sensitive about the welfare of their dogs.

But the dog is less than popular in the cycling world. Popular magazines and books frequently detail rather frightening variations on the classic bicycle-dog confrontation. Often such detail is followed by suggestions for defense against attacking dogs, including the use of air horns, ammonia water, "mace," clubs, whips, whistles, dog repellant, and other assorted items.

The tourist who arms to defend against dogs, and uses any

armament freely, stands to lose goodwill among local residents in rural areas. Bicycles are strange-looking and sounding contraptions to both local dogs and residents when one travels "back of beyond," and a wise cyclist will try to keep the goodwill of both.

The response to a dog chasing a bicycle should be appropriate: not overreacting with the use of heavy artillery against merely scared or curious animals, but protecting one's self against injury while respecting the rights of the dog and the feelings of the local inhabitants.

Whether dogs bark in German, English, or Japanese, their reactions to bicycles are universal. A wise cyclist learns to anticipate the actions of a loose dog, and tries to avoid any conflict with the animal or the owner. The first defense is speed. Dogs are strictly short-distance sprinters — few will chase you more than 200 yards. Dogs instinctively attack from the rear; while they maneuver, you make your fast break. As a last resort, get out the air pump and tap Fido with a short, controlled swing on his sensitive snout. If all else fails, dismount, get the bike between you and the dog, or use the bike as a weapon to discourage further attack.

Lightly traveled roads often have chickens, ducks, and geese on or near the highway. A passing bicycle seems to terrify such fowl more than motorized vehicles. This may be because of the relatively silent approach of the bicycle. Chickens tend to do sudden and not very bright things, like darting across the road for the chicken coop in front of an approaching vehicle. Hitting a chicken, despite the dubious humor involved, is a serious matter. I have several scars to show for my one collision with a hen. Chickens also seem to hide in the weeds with several friends. Therefore, the sudden appearance of one chicken might well indicate the presence of several.

Ducks are a different story, since they appear to move in a more reasonable (and slower) manner. Geese aren't generally found on roads, but are more aggressive and will bite.

Horses and other draft animals are used extensively for work and transportation in areas other than the urbanized United States. In many rural areas of this country, as well, a bicyclist should expect to be involved in the age-old bicycle/ horse confrontation. It is important to remember that cyclists were originally denounced by horse owners for excessive speed and frightening their animals, and the same situation exists today wherever the two modes of transportation must co-exist. Horses are high-strung animals and should be passed at the slowest possible speed, and as far away as reasonable. Since a horse may not notice or be aware of a bicycle's approach until the last minute, it is the responsibility of the cyclist to exercise all due caution.

Since many pedestrians depend on the sound of vehicles approaching them from the rear or at crossroads, the silent cyclist should shout out a warning to back-packers or others walking ahead. In areas of the world not plagued by incessant motorized traffic, caution is needed to warn of your approach. Use a bell. It's a dignified and useful way of saying "I'm on the road — be careful."

Road Conditions

A "lay-over road" is a highway that has one center lane paved wide enough for one car. Isolated areas of the US and many back roads (or main roads) throughout the world have one-lane paved roads. When approaching cars meet on such a road, each "lays over" onto the unpaved shoulder of the road with its right wheels while leaving its left wheels on the pavement. It is rather interesting to watch drivers used to such roads whip their cars around one another in a cloud of dust while waving with one hand.

This type of road is potentially dangerous for cyclists. Most cars and trucks drive as though these are one-way roads until they see an approaching vehicle. Since bicycles are not as visible as larger vehicles, safety demands that a cyclist be highly visible. In addition, many vehicles will not lay-over for a bicycle. In many cases, the drop off from the pavement to the dirt is rather large, and this could well create a hazardous situation.

With sustained traffic, lay-over roads become extremely uncomfortable bicycle routes. Most often this type of road will be lightly traveled, but heavy traffic will obviously create problems for cyclists and such highways should be avoided at all cost.

Many rural routes around the world are surfaced by spreading tar and then compressing rock into it. This makes a decent light-duty surface which tends to melt at high temperatures. Tar will then run to the surface and will stick to bicycle tires, making a mess. There is really very little that can be done about this except to try to avoid the soft spots. This is an extremely common form of paving that pre-dates more modern forms, and it will be found throughout the world. About the only way to avoid this problem is to sit out the hot part of the day underneath a convenient tree.

"Washboard" is the effect of heavy vehicles braking or cornering on light-duty surfaces, or the effect of concentrated braking on heavy-duty asphalt. Ripples appear in the surface of the road, and a bicycle can experience extreme control problems when entering affected areas at high speeds.

Look for washboard in any slow-down areas, such as approaches to stop signs and sharp curves. It is a particular hazard at the bottoms of hills, inside steep or sharp curves, and along the uphill approaches to sharp curves. All such areas will be subject to wash-boarding, and should be approached with caution.

In order to avoid these ripples, the cyclist should stay as high in a banked curve as possible. Since braking is difficult in washboarded areas, stops should be made very gradually in such areas with the bulk of the braking done before entering the affected portion of the highway.

Because cyclists and trains often seek the same water grade through hills and mountains, cyclists must often deal with relatively unimproved railroad grade crossings. The danger at such crossings cannot be overemphasized. They could well be the greatest cause of single bicycle accidents. And the further from the protected environment of well-maintained main highways one gets, the greater hazard such crossings represent.

There is one virtually accident-free method of getting across any railroad crossing: walk the bicycle. If there is the least doubt about the safety of the crossing, the cyclist should dismount and walk. The expense in time is more than outweighed by the potential disaster of falling on the rails.

When crossing tracks, either walking or riding, each rail must be approached at a right angle. If it is raining, exercise the utmost caution — "cross at a crawl." The front wheel must not be turned while the bike is on the track. Any track that crosses a highway diagonally must be crossed at right angles, even if that means cutting across the road to do so (just don't cross diagonally into the path of oncoming traffic — that's rarely very safe).

Crossings must be taken slowly if they are unimproved. Low speed decreases stability, of course, but also lessens the force of the fall if the bike does go down, and gives you a chance of falling on a low-priority part of your bicycle or body. In addition, poorly maintained crossings can injure rims and/or tires if the crossing is done at speed.

In the event that a railroad crossing is taken at high speed, by design or accident, the cyclist should get up off the saddle slightly, putting weight on pedals, handle bars, and seat. The tracks must be approached at right angles, and no braking should be done while crossing. Concentrate on simply keeping the bike upright and at right angles to the tracks.

The groove beside a rail can swallow a bicycle tire and throw a rider with astounding speed. A Volkswagen was actually flipped when its front tire dropped into a next-to-rail groove in San Francisco. The many, oft-times unmarked, railroad crossings found on the back roads of the world are deserving of respect as one of the most dangerous road hazards faced by a cyclist.

Like railroad crossings, rural bridges are worthy of much caution. Even bridges on main roads are often poorly maintained and quite rough in some areas of the world. There are two basic problems on back-road bridges. The first is that they are generally one-lane. This requires the cyclist to assert his rights to the road, while protecting himself against those who would ignore his existence.

The second problem is that the bridge is often wooden and extremely rough. There may well be quite a gap between floorboards or between the bridge and the highway. It is also common to have a drop-off from the bridge to the highway. All of these conditions require caution.

The proper technique to use in approaching any back-road stream crossing is to slow before the bridge, determine whether it is rough enough to require slow-speed crossing, and then move decisively to act on that judgment.

Crossing at high speed should be done with weight distributed to pedals and handlebars. Initial drop-offs from the bridge to the road level may be "jumped," but the bicycle must be kept in a straight line and braking should not be attempted while on a rough bridge. Low-speed crossing is safer, of course, but requires loss of momentum for possible approaching grades in hilly country.

Some bridges are just not made for bicycles; in a high-traffic situation with no shoulder clearance and dangerous expansion joints, never take chances — get off, walk, and enjoy the view. Some rural roads have signs warning of approaching fords. Some do not. A series of fords on a downhill run makes for serious braking problems.

The particular hazard of unpaved roads is sliding. Loose

The international tourist, or the US tourist who seeks something more exciting than US 36 across Kansas, will end up on unpaved roads. And, from necessity, he will develop a whole technique for riding loose-surfaced roads. The Sunday rider can simply slow down for the short sections of dirt that he might ride, but the tourist looking for the essence of his own or a foreign country will end up on unpaved highways for mile upon mile.

Unpaved roads combine every road hazard — washboard, narrowness, poor bridges or fords, loose surface, steep grades — and present a definite challenge to a tourist. At the same time, they offer access to areas of the US and other countries not seen by the average visitor.

The essence of success on such a road is outstanding control over the bicycle. And such control is learned only by riding very slowly through the washboard loose surfaces. A tourist who would ride abroad with confidence must put a little dust and mud on his machine. The unpaved roads of the world offer some of the finest riding, but at times also are the ultimate test of skill and equipment.

Some rural roads, particularly the gravel-tar type, will often have loose gravel on the surface. This condition is most common in winter and spring when spinning tires have thrown gravel on the surface, but is found year-round on sharp curves and steep grades. This condition is often associated with washboarding, making a dangerous combination.

Gravel areas must be anticipated, as little braking or steering can be done once you're "in the soup." In most cases automobile tires will have cleared a path through, and this should be followed with caution.

Like bridges and railroad crossings, chuckholed and broken areas should be run at low speeds. The most important rule in keeping control is to not attempt any drastic changes in direction or speed while passing over rough pavement.

I fear chickens second only to double trailers. I always

wear cycling gloves so that the roadway might eat up leather
instead of my palms as I slide along in a burst of feathers.

Passport to Freedom

by Lloyd Sumner

I have just completed a four-year, 28,478-mile bicycle trip around the world, had a wonderful time, learned a lot, and returned with more money than when I started. I actually began my trip as the result of a logical exercise. I hadn't even taken an overnight trip by bicycle before I started.

It all began some time ago when I did some research on endangered species of animals and came to the conclusion that all wild animals ought to be free. After thinking about it for a moment I could find no reason why I should be an exception. Freedom would involve being able to move about physically, mentally, and spiritually, being of no bother to any other people, and not being dependent on any other people.

I was keen to learn first hand about other countries, cultures, and most of all, about myself. Now after four years of continual travel on the bike, learning and enjoying, I'm convinced that if you have the time and a capacity for letting things come to you, each in its own way, the bicycle is the ultimate mode of travel.

Consider many of the usual ways of moving through different countries—car, bus, train, motorcycle. All are an "abstraction" of movement. They remove you from the lands and the people. In a car, the panorama goes by like a slow-motion film. You, the traveler, are uninvolved, merely a spectator enduring a period of time between a start and finish, experiencing a country as a series of terminals instead of truly encountering the infinite distinctiveness of the area you are visiting.

Consider also that motorized travel contributes to the rape

of the earth's resources. It creates noise and spews pollution. In much the same way, hitchhiking is ultimately frustrating; and it ties you into dependencies on others.

● The bicycle takes me over any road I choose and gives me access to spaces off the road I wish to explore.

● It's a people-to-people machine. You are open, flexible, accessible and appealing, especially in many Third World countries where economics results in a majority use of bicycles for daily transportation.

● By traveling in "bicycle time," I physically and emotionally experience the land, hearing, seeing, smelling, feeling the terrain with all my muscles, nerves and senses.

● Using the bicycle keeps me fit and healthy.

● Moving by bike is environmentally perfect—it leaves no wastes and makes no noise.

● The bike is easy to maintain.

● When I have to, the bicycle is easy to take on planes and boats. It's also easy to conceal it when I wish to move on foot.

● It offers me a continual source of adventure on a budget I can afford.

● It not only allows me communion with the land and people I visit, but gives me a sense of the perfection of things, and of belonging to the moments I travel.

Once a person commits himself to finding and experiencing the many harmonies in life (and the bicycle is an excellent way of "tuning" you into them), nature seems to "unite" with him. For example, during the four years I've been traveling, I had only 15 days of bad weather. Even while cycling around the British Isles, I enjoyed sunshine every day. The farmers in Ireland blamed me for their driest summer in 100 years.

I felt these things about traveling by bike before I started and they were confirmed as I moved along. From country to country I found welcome — and *respect.* I had no trouble with police or customs (34 countries visited). I was never robbed or assaulted. Despite 28,478 miles of slightly daredevilish cycling

Southeast Asia offers many contrasts to the touring cyclist. Ornate Buddhist temples in Bangkok are examples of an ancient but enduring culture. In the countryside, elephants are still used for heavy labor. Climbing up for a ride, native-style, can be hair-raising. (Lloyd Sumner)

(I won't get off the pavement for anybody) and another 4000 miles of other self-propelled travel (including climbing the highest peaks on four continents), I haven't been injured. But on one occasion I *was* sick.

(That one flaw to an otherwise perfect tour happened in a remote part of Java. Fortunately, I was staying with a family and didn't have to go anywhere. Ever since the early morning, my head had been pounding fiercely. My insides felt like I had swallowed a porcupine. Each way I moved brought me intense pain. I had a fever and even a rare case of diarrhea. There were no western doctors or medicine. By midafternoon the elderly servant, who had no education but was a practicing folk doctor, asked if I'd like her to make me well. Ready to consider

anything, I quickly said yes. She rushed off to gather various herbs and unmentionable ingredients to make an ointment which she scraped into my naked back with the sharp edge of an old Chinese coin. Within five minutes of her finishing this *kerokan* I was completely well. Headache was gone. Porcupine was gone. Fever was gone. Even the diarrhea was gone.)

To stay healthy it is necessary to use a certain caution. Don't think that just because the natives don't get sick under the prevailing conditions, you won't. You don't have their many years of building up resistances. To be totally safe don't eat any food unless it has been cooked or peeled (i.e., no salads). You can't get away from the bacteria altogether but with a strong, healthy body you will have few problems. Enterovioform clears up a normal case of diarrhea fairly quickly. I got so I could eat most any food without a problem, but I never got so I could drink the water. Most of my liquid came in the form of tea or Coke. If these were not available, I tried to boil the water or use halazone tablets.

Try to get your necessary shots in western countries, if possible. One of my most traumatic experiences was when I had to get a cholera shot in Katmandu. Having heard of numerous cases of hepatitis from an unclean needle, I bought a new needle for my shot. Apparently the doctor had never seen a new needle before because he jabbed it into my arm without removing the protective wire inside. He strained and grunted but just couldn't get the serum into my arm. Finally he removed it and held the needle in the air and squeezed with both hands. The needle exploded. Not having time to get another, I had to trust his well-used ones but insisted on a long sterilization bath. The doctor tried to remove my concern as his technician removed the needle from the sterilizer. I watched the technician drop the needle on the dirty floor, pick it up with his fingers and hand it to the doctor. They thought I was being fussy when I insisted it be sterilized again. But eventually I got a shot that didn't make me sick.

In Australia, I ran across my first emu. It raised itself to its full height and then attacked my camera. I had to resort to an old trick to get it away. In emu society, the tallest is the boss. By raising my hand over my head I became taller and it backed away. (Lloyd Sumner)

To help avoid difficulty with food, I tried to prepare myself in advance by eating all kinds of unusual foods, making a specialty of wild foods. This, I'm sure, along with good health generally, accounted for my lack of trouble adjusting to different diets. One Indonesian family served me a breakfast of a perfectly intact pig brain on a bowl of rice. Still another served goat intestines and sheep testicles and other slimy, strange-textured delicacies which I didn't attempt to identify. All these I ate with great enjoyment and no ill effects.

One does have to watch his manners, however. Normally I had to remember to touch no food with my left hand (used by Asians instead of toilet paper), to leave some food on my plate

After a long ride through the back country of New Zealand, the only way forward was over this bridge which was being repaired. I had to do some tricky maneuvering to avoid a 30 foot drop into the river. (Lloyd Sumner)

to show that there had been enough, and to belch loudly when I had finished — to show that I had enjoyed the meal.

Language is not such a big problem. One can get along with just English more easily in Asia and Africa than in much of rural Europe. Even so, it's worth learning a few key words. Especially learn to count and to ask the prices of various items. Sign language or drawing a picture will usually get you what you want if all else fails. But not always. In one remote part of Indonesia the local people didn't even speak Indonesian. Sign language left them much amused and my drawn picture was accepted as a present and rushed off to show the neighbors. The more you know of the language of the area, the more you will get out of the trip.

On the financial side of perpetual travel — it is necessary to be wealthy. But let me give you a new definition of the word. Wealthy is having more than you need. This is normally interpreted as having an endless supply of money to buy an endless supply of goods and services. But it is far easier to reduce your needs rather than increase your bank account.

I began my trip with $200 in my pocket and enough money in the bank to get me home from any place in the world in case I couldn't handle it anymore. I returned with more than the $200 in my pocket and my savings still intact. I didn't take normal employment at any time during the trip (except for a month as a crewman on a yacht) and had no sponsorship. But because I need so little, I can easily earn what I require by giving lectures and slide shows, appearing on radio and television, and writing for newspapers and magazines.

Besides having an unusual and adventurous trip, it is useful to become an expert. It can be almost anything – wildlife, flower arranging, bridges, native houses, counter culture, farming techniques, etc. By gathering information and pictures about your subject in every place visited, you soon become a "world expert" and can always find an audience for an illustrated talk.

Most of the roads in New Zealand are fairly well-made. But to get to the most beautiful country, you sometimes have to use roads like this one. (Lloyd Sumner)

You don't have to go all the way to the Antarctic to see wild penguins. I saw this one on Shag Point in New Zealand. (Lloyd Sumner)

To facilitate making contacts, I published and distributed a leaflet which described briefly my trip and what I had to offer. It gained me much hospitality as well, and was even accepted by some countries in lieu of an onward air ticket as proof that I'd be leaving the country.

Numerous people I met indicated a desire to keep up with my adventure, so I started my own newsletter. *Lloyd's Trail-O-Gram* was published monthly for the last 3½ years and was sent to anyone willing to contribute $5-10 a year. I never made any money on it, although I could have if I'd had a better distribution system. But it was useful in other ways. Some people say it is like reading a book as it is being written. No one, not even the author, knows how it will end. Others say it is so much better to read about it while it is, rather than when it was.

I keep intending to also publish a small booklet containing highlights of my adventures to date, to sell as I go along. Although as yet untested, I think this idea could be a good way to make an extended trip pay for itself.

The real secret is making your money go farther. By living cheaply, you don't have to pay taxes. That alone cuts about 20% off the price of everything. Since you are going by bicycle, transportation costs are minimal. If you have patience and persistence, ocean voyages can often be made as a crewman on a yacht, though it is getting hard to find work on a freighter. Local foods in the interesting parts of the world (Europe not included) are much cheaper than in your home town. On remote and beautiful Lake Toba in Sumatra I couldn't eat 75 cents' worth of food in a day, and I'm a big eater. Accommodation almost everywhere can be considerably less than you are now paying for an apartment.

It is absolutely necessary to price everything before agreeing to buy. Otherwise you are likely to be charged considerably more. In Bali I sometimes got a meal for 13 cents if I asked first. Once I decided to be more trusting and not ask. I was charged 95 cents.

Bali provides a good example of two different ways of traveling. The typical tourist will stay at the Bali Hai Hotel for $32/day, pay $6 for a meal, lie on an ugly beach that's unsafe for swimming, and be totally shielded from the Balinese. Seven miles away is Kuta Beach, far more beautiful and safe for swimming. Clean private rooms with bath are $1/day and a huge variety of delicious (even western) food is available for less than 50 cents a meal. From the veranda outside my door, I looked into a Balinese family compound where barebreasted women and naked children worked and ran about, continuing their age-old life style seemingly unconcerned with the white-skinned intruder.

In Nepal, more money doesn't buy the best experience. One can trek with an organized group for $25/day, live in tents and eat western food. You see the mountains but you don't experience the people. Or you can go as I did, staying with families and eating their food at a cost of no more than 60 cents a day. The families always seemed eager to take me in. The few rupees represented a small fortune to them. The sleeping was usually on a goatskin or bamboo mat with the rest of the family and often with all their goats and chickens.

When buying clothes, choose easily washable fabrics and wash them yourself. It is easy. A little hand soap, water and elbow grease do the job. Clothes are either practical or symbolic. Choose only the symbolic kind and buy them at second-hand shops.

My wardrobe consists of one pair of wool trousers, one pair of cotton shorts, two shirts, three identical socks (wash one each night and keep rotating), one change of underwear and a sun hat. Anything more than that is dead weight unless the weather is cold. In that case I just add a layer of wool.

Toiletries should consist of a toothbrush. I further allow myself the luxury of a razor. (A neat appearance is helpful in getting through customs and being accepted by the local people.) Hand soap carried for clothes washing makes a good lather. Aftershave lotion, toothpaste, deodorant, shampoo, and any form of make-up are unnecessary and of no value. Continued pursuit of vanity inhibits any chance of personal spiritual growth.

Other items worth carrying are a lightweight tent (mine weighs one pound but kept me dry in a hurricane in Hawaii), an Ensolite pad, and a lightweight down-filled sleeping bag (mine weighs 2.2 pounds but kept me warm at 18,700 feet in the Himalayas). Other equipment needed for special side trips can usually be borrowed, rented or bought and resold. I carried a simple first aid kit but never used it except for a headache pill or sunburn cream for my lower lip.

My permanent travel equipment also includes a set of slides to show to people who offer me hospitality, and for lectures. And of course a camera to take more pictures. A small, automatic-metering, fixed-lens camera in the $100 range is sufficient. If you want to make the natives very happy, carry a Polaroid and give them a picture of themselves, preferably with you in it too. For ease of taking photos of natives carry prints of other natives in different lands. Most will then be proud to be in your collection.

Your bicycle should be rugged and well-geared. The advantages of a super lightweight bike are lost when luggage is added. It is much better to have a bike that isn't likely to break down on some lonely desert; simply add lower gears to help pull the extra weight uphill. A spare tube, gear and brake cables, and a few tools (adjustable wrench, pliers, screwdriver, tire tools, patching kit) should be carried.

Be aware that airlines will normally carry a bicycle for free if total weight is under 44 pounds (I've flown with my bike 17 times and haven't yet been charged for excess weight although I'm always several pounds over), but trains, buses and ships usually do charge extra. Airlines sometimes make an "awkward handling" charge of a few dollars for bicycles carried within a country (e.g., between California and Hawaii).

That, then, is all you need to take with you, but you must be careful or you'll spend a lot replacing things stolen. In some countries three out of every four travelers I met had been robbed. One guy was robbed twice and almost a third time in one day. I escaped, I think, by always looking poor and being extra observant. I carried passport, money, tickets and any other valuables in a cloth money belt worn inside my pants. If sleeping in a public place I put money belt and camera in the bottom of my sleeping bag. At least half of your funds should be carried in cash, as travellers' checks are *not* accepted everywhere and are not worth as much on the black market.

A good lock is a deterrent for potential bike thieves for *short* times. At night, I always took my bike in the room with me or used it as a support for my tent. If I had to leave it fully

loaded in the city (for example, to get a visa), I left it in front
of a restaurant window. Any potential thief assumed I was
sitting just across the glass. I carried no insurance of any kind
on anything throughout the trip and didn't regret it.

Only once did I get careless – but once is usually too
often. I had been carrying my money belt in a special pocket of
my pack (usually safe enough while cycling) and had apparently
neglected to zip it. Moving fast through the flatlands of
southern Nepal, a truck passed and the driver waved me down.
He shouted something in Hindi and pointed back up the road. I
soon realized that my money belt was gone. With the road lined
with people, there seemed no chance of recovering it. Before
complete panic grabbed me a young man cycled alongside, my
money belt, completely intact, in his hand. I couldn't believe
my eyes. Was this really Asia? The man could have sold my
passport and cashed my checks on the Katmandu black market
and probably retired for life. I offered him a reward but he
refused. "I am just proud that I could be help to you."

*Bicycle repairmen on Fiji are always eager to serve. (Lloyd
Sumner)*

Photographing elephants, even work elephants in Thailand, can be risky. This one chased me for three miles after I took this picture. (Lloyd Sumner)

In crowded areas I usually prefer not to camp. But fortunately, cheap rooms are usually available. All over Southeast Asia, hotels which cost less than a dollar a night can be found in most towns. Otherwise I stayed in police stations where I was always made welcome. In Thailand I stayed in Buddhist temples. In India I stayed in DAK bungalows — a four-room suite which was clean, comfortable, and most of all private — for $1.10/night. In Australia I stayed with private families all but seven nights during my first three months there. The people of New Zealand and South Africa are also very hospitable, but in the British Isles and Europe I had to resort to continual camping unless I had contacts from a previous trip. When camping in western countries I simply get out of sight. If I fear trouble, I camp in a cemetery or ask a farmer for permission to camp on his land. This permission is almost always granted and is often accompanied with an invitation to the evening meal. When it isn't safe or legal to build an open fire, I use a tiny solid-paraffin army-type stove. It only weighs a few ounces and causes no worry over spilled fuel.

Don't worry in advance too much about the details of your trip. The best information on conditions, customs, worthwhile things to do in a country comes from other travelers. A good atlas — found in libraries everywhere — gives climatic and season information. The "Travel Information Manual" possessed by all travel agents gives the latest information on entrance requirements of countries, etc. Government tourist bureaus are sometimes helpful.

I try to be aware of the coming seasons and the best time to be in certain places but am always ready to change my plans if some new opportunity comes along. Sometimes good things happen almost accidentally. Like my string of five full moons. The first came with me camped near the base of Mt. Everest and magically transformed the high Himalayas. Exactly 28 days later I watched the full moon illuminate the Taj Mahal. The next full moon came while I was on board the ship between Bombay and Mombassa and was especially pretty reflecting off the ocean. The best one of all came the following month and lit my climb the last 4000 feet of Mt. Kilamanjaro. I arrived on top in time to see the full moon set just before the sun rose over the horizon 170 miles away. Another cycle of the full moon and I'd arrived at Victoria Falls, the moon forming a moonbow in the mist.

If you want the full measure of the experience, go alone. If you are willing to halve it, take along a friend. I have only felt lonely when I've been in a crowd of people with no way to talk to them. At those times when hundreds of eyes are watching my every move, it would have been nice to talk to someone understanding. Actually I'm considering taking a companion along on my next world trip — traveling by a great variety of means instead of *just* by bicycle. Applications for an adventurous, intelligent, no hang-ups, got-it-all-together female are now open.

2

EXPLORING EUROPE

by Clifford Graves

Although my first bicycle tour in a foreign country was hardly a three-star achievement, it did earn me a medal for performance above and beyond the call of duty.

I had arrived in England shortly after Pearl Harbor as commanding officer of a surgical unit. I noticed immediately that the English nation moved on wheels — bicycle wheels. Thousands of riders passed my window at Cowley Barracks, not far from Oxford. Gliding silently through the murk and gloom, they looked like a long line of ghosts on their way to the nether regions. Finally, I could stand it no longer. I hurried over to Halford's on the High.

"Can you sell me a bicycle?" I asked with some trepidation.

"A bicycle? You mean a *new* bicycle? Impossible. Don't you know there is a war on?" He gave me a wan smile.

"Well, I should. I am a lot farther from home than you."

"How would you like a used bicycle?" He showed me an

ancient hack with a frame too large, a handlebar too high, and a
saddle too wide.

"What's that big hub in the back?" I asked.

"It's a speed gear," he said. "When it's working, you have
three speeds. Actually, only two in this case. The third one is
out, and we can't make repairs."

"Why not?"

"Because the Sturmey Archer people are making tanks
instead of hubgears."

"OK. I'll buy it."

Congratulating myself on my acquisition, I rode back to
the barracks through a torrential rain. In spite of being
drenched, I felt a delicious sense of freedom.

After a few preliminary excursions around the neighbor-
hood, I began to toy with the idea of a tour. I studied the map.
Maybe I could get all the way to Stratford. It was 40 miles
away.

The road from Oxford to Stratford leads through the
Cotswolds. Today, that road is jammed with cars, but during
the war, it was deserted. All roads in England were deserted.
Drastic gas rationing had eliminated every trace of motor traffic
except for an occasional army truck. Imagine the peace and
quiet.

That night I stayed in a delightful hotel, the Swan in
Stratford, and the next day I started back. Emboldened by my
success, I now chose the lanes which took me through villages
like Shipston on the Stour and Moreton on the Marsh. I began
to feel some raindrops when only halfway. Unconsciously, I
increased my pace. Everything went well till noon. Then the
strain began to tell.

Having skipped breakfast in my haste to get away, I began
to suffer from a bad case of what is called the bonk in England
and the sags in America, lowered blood sugar. In this unhappy
state, the wheels feel dead, the saddle hits wrong, the chain is
sluggish and the gears won't mesh. The muscles ache, the legs

won't move, the head gets dizzy, the eyes focus and you are overcome by the pain of monotony as much as by the monotony of pain. I slowed to a crawl.

I became aware of a rider behind me. It was a girl, and pretty at that. But instead of slowing, she shot by like a gazelle. That did it. If I could not keep up with a girl, I'd quit. I got off and massaged the unwilling legs. Maybe a bicycle was not so wonderful after all.

After a rest, I shifted into low gear and started up a long hill. Then a swift descent, and at the bottom, who should be standing by the side of the road but the same girl. Her bike was leaning against a tree and she was looking disconsolately at the chain on the ground. She had lost the master link. In those days, every chain was held together by a horseshoe-shaped piece of metal that had an annoying tendency to work loose and drop off. The link usually rolled into the grass where you had no more chance of finding it than a dime at the bottom of a swimming pool.

I stopped and asked if I could help. Even in her drab ATS uniform, the girl was charming. With a sparkle in her eye, a wave in her hair, and a flush on her cheeks, she had a natural beauty that came through without rouge, paint or lipstick. We looked for the lost link but without success. Then I remembered that the man at Halford's had given me an extra link. "Take this," he had said, "you never know. No charge." Digging the link from the depths of my saddle bag, I offered it to the girl. It slid into place without fuss or fumble. If I hadn't been bald and bashful, I think she would have kissed me. She just looked at me with those big eyes, and then she was off. I never saw her again.

The payoff came later. Towards evening, when I was still miles from home on a lonely road, I came to another hill. I mustered my last bit of energy, bore down on the pedals, and bang! There went my own chain.

On a bicycle trip you never know what is going to happen

next. That is one of its attractions. If you are always well-fed and well-bedded, you become bored. If you are always comfortable, you no longer appreciate it. If you are always seeing the same people, you take them for granted. On a bicycle trip, you meet new situations all the time. I'll never forget an encounter in the Black Forest.

I was traveling in a remote area of the Breg Valley. After losing my way, I was overtaken by darkness. At last I came on a small chalet that stood by itself in a dense woods. It looked as if it might be a *Gasthaus*, so I walked in. My guess was right. I found myself in a small *Bierstube* where a few of the locals had gathered for their schnapps. They were being served by a handsome woman in a dirndl dress. She had the high cheek bones of the Slav with long, wavy, blonde hair and a peaches-and-cream complexion. I asked if she would have a room for me. She looked me over closely, then smiled.

"Jawohl."

"Thank goodness," I said. "I thought I might have to spend the night in the open."

"I am busy here now," she said. "Go up to the head of the stairs and take room number three."

I found the room, changed into clean clothes, and went back downstairs. The bar was empty now. Over schnapps, I learned that the woman was really from Estonia. She had married a German before the war, and they had bought the hotel. During the war, the husband had been killed at Stalingrad. Without any other source of income, she had to run the hotel herself. But business was poor, she said. In post-war Germany, nobody had money.

Later that evening, she served me a dinner of sausages and potatoes while waiting on a few drop-ins. In between, she came over to my table to talk. "The war was devastating," she said, "and it was all in vain. What was left at the end, the French took when they occupied the area. You Americans are strange. First, you devastate the country and then you rebuild it. If not for the Marshall Plan, we would be destitute." She sighed.

The bar was empty now. Now and then she got up to stir the fire. There was no other source of heat, and the temperature away from the fire dropped perceptibly. I shivered.

"It's going to be cold upstairs," I said.

"Yes," she said, looking me straight in the eye. "But I would be glad to keep you warm."

I stayed a week.

Over the Bars & Into Europe

The most important thing to remember when deciding where to tour is that traffic on the main roads in Europe is just as noisy, disruptive, and jarring as in America, if not more so. European cars are underpowered by our standards. That means the engine is always straining. The noise is dreadful. In addition, the gasoline is heavily doctored, so exhaust fumes smell even worse than they do here. The combination of noise and smell destroys all pleasure for the person on a bicycle. A day on a main road in Europe shatters the nerves, chokes the lungs, and deafens the ears.

I am making a big point of this because it is not sufficiently stressed in the existing books on the subject. Only a few months ago I received the following letter from a couple in New Jersey:

"Last September we planned a tour based on one described in (a well-known book). We started from the Milan airport, followed the shore of Lake Maggiore, entered Switzerland, and eventually came back to Italy. After seven days, we had to give up. Traffic wiped us out.

"There is only one road around the lake, and it is jammed. At times the traffic was so bad that the road became positively dangerous. There just wasn't any shoulder. At many places, the roadside was set off by curbing or fences, trapping a cyclist. Double trailer-trucks are used extensively. Italians have the small-car philosophy. Full bore is the only speed.

"Edith took a tumble when a double trailer-truck charged by at 40 miles an hour. Fortunately she suffered only cuts and bruises. The bike escaped also. But it could have been worse, much worse. According to the people we spoke to, traffic on these roads never lets up. It is an all-year condition. No one cycles there. I hope other people do not attempt a tour of the Italian lakes."

When planning a tour, you must first be sure that you will find plenty of suitable roads. Not all countries have them in abundance. The best are France, England, Belgium, the Netherlands, and Germany in that order. Also very suitable are the Scandinavian countries, Switzerland, Austria and Czechoslovakia. Countries to be avoided are Spain, Italy, Hungary, Yugoslavia, Bulgaria, and Greece. Here, the little roads, if you can find them, are too rough.

I find that many prospective cycle tourists have a tendency to regard a bicycle tour the same as a tour by car. "We want to see London, Amsterdam and Paris," is a typical comment. "And we plan to cycle all the way." The sad truth is that it is no fun to cycle from London to Amsterdam to Paris because you cannot avoid main roads in the limited time you have. The answer is to choose a few areas with good cycling and go there by train.

So where are the good cycling areas? I will list a few, but I want to stress that it will mean little unless you have at least a general idea of geography. Before you can make an intelligent decision to tour Brittany, for instance, you must know where Brittany is. Overall orientation comes first. For this purpose, get a book of maps such as the Hallwag Auto Atlas. It can be bought at most automobile clubs and at larger bookstores. The Hallwag Atlas covers Europe (except for Russia) in 90 maps in a format of 6 by 9 inches and on a scale of one to a million. It is a book to be studied at home, not to be taken with you on tour. For actual navigation, you need maps with greater detail. I will say a little more about them in a moment.

After you have acquainted yourself with the general geography, you are ready to study the following list of good cycling areas:

In England: the South Downs, Devon and Cornwall, the Cotswolds, north Wales, Yorkshire and the lake district. In Scotland, the western Highlands. In Ireland, the west and southwest.

In Holland, everywhere. In Belgium, the border zone with Germany. In Luxemburg, everywhere.

In Germany, anywhere south of the line Cologne-Kassel. Especially recommended: the Moselle Valley and the Black Forest. The Rhine Valley is crowded. It is better done by boat. In Denmark, everywhere. In Sweden, the lakes in the southern part of the country. In Norway, the fjords. Start in Bergen.

In France, everywhere except the north. Especially recommended are the Loire Valley, Brittany, the Vosges, Burgundy, the Massif Central and the Pyrenees. The Riviera is beautiful but crowded. The little roads are fine but the coast is bedlam. Strong riders can tackle the French Alps by starting in Nice and going north over the small roads closest to the Italian border. In doing so, you climb six passes over 7000 feet: the Restefond, the Vars, the Izoard, the Lautaret, the Galibier, and the Iseran.

In Switzerland you have to be selective. Don't get caught on a major pass in the high season. Cars will kill you. The Jura Mountains on the border with France are superb. It is often possible to avoid busy stretches by taking the train. The country has unlimited possibilities but only after a careful study of a detailed map.

In Austria you have very much the same problem. In the mountains, all traffic is channeled on major roads which are often the only ones available. However, if you take the trouble to study detailed maps, you can find smaller roads about half the time. The scenery everywhere is magnificent, and the people are extremely friendly or *gemuetlich*. At one time, Swissair ran bicycle tours based on Graz. This area is not as mountainous.

Once you are on the road, you need maps with greater detail than the "one-to-a-million" series. I recommend that you buy these maps overseas rather than here. For one thing, the maps I am talking about are not easy to find in America, and for another, they are expensive.

You need these maps in such numbers that they quickly become a burden to carry. My system is to buy the detailed maps not more than six at a time and send them home when you enter a new area. I now have a five-foot shelf of maps. Never throw a map away. They are your best memento.

I once met an American couple on the road in France. They were navigating by a single map on a scale of one to a million. As a result, they had missed all the beautiful little sideroads. When I asked them why they had not bought the proper maps, they said it was the expense. True, a detailed map covering barely 50 miles now costs close to a dollar. But that dollar is very little when you consider that the map is your key to a different world. Compared with the overall cost of a tour, maps are a minor expense.

It is indeed sad that so many Americans come back from Europe without ever seeing what lies beyond the main road. It is doubly sad when a *cyclist* comes back without seeing what lies beyond the main road. And yet it happens. Not only do main roads suffer from the inevitable commercialism but they also destroy all sense of intimacy. It is only on the little road that you taste the true flavor. Here is where you find the peaceful village, the unsullied countryside, the natural beauty. And here is where the people are glad to see you.

So what about the detailed maps? They are mostly on a scale of 1 to 200,000, and you buy them in bookstores. In England, ask for the Bartholomew series, half-inch to the mile.

Detailed maps will help you find the little roads and cycle paths, like this one in the Wye Valley, which show you the true character of a country. (Bernard Thompson)

That comes to a scale of 1 to 126,720. Today, these maps are gradually being replaced with maps of 1 to 100,000 but it will be some time before the conversion is complete. "Barts" maps are also sold by the Cyclists Touring Club, 69 Meadrow, Godalming, Surrey, England.

In France, use the Michelin maps on a scale of 1 to 200,000. In Germany, the comparable map is issued by the Shell Company under the name of *Deutsche Generalkarte*. It is also on a scale of 1 to 200,000. In Holland, cyclists use the maps issued by their touring organizations, the *Koninklijke Nederlandsche Toeristenbond* with headquarters at 5 Museumplein in Amsterdam. These maps are on a scale of 1 to 100,000 and they cost nearly $4 apiece but they are so explicit that it is a pleasure to look at them. In other countries, you should ask for maps on that scale or as close to it as possible. Without these maps, you never find the cycle paths that the country is famous for.

In the appendix I describe six recommended tours in some detail. Clip these pages and take them with you when you go to Europe for the first time. You might find yourself near the areas. Reading the itineraries without a map is a waste of time.

Three Styles of Travel

On your bicycle, you have a choice of three styles of travel: camping, hosteling and hotels. A few words about each:

Camping is the choice of the person who wants to be free and independent. You need a tent, a stove, a cookset, and a sleeping bag. All of this weighs at least 10 pounds over your normal load. Camping in Europe usually means using established campsites, which have a tendency to be noisy, crowded and commercialized. In return, you get facilities like showers, laundromats, and quick-lunch counters. These camp sites are usually indicated on the map. If not, they can be found if you ask. The charge for two people runs from two to four dollars. This is about the same as you would pay in a hostel.

The purists stay away from established campsites.

Impatient with the organized disorganization of the sites, they make their own. Simply pitch your tent when you see a good spot. The main disadvantage is that you probably won't have water at your doorstep. Looking for a good site, pitching your tent, and cooking out take time and you have to cut down on your cycling to some extent. But these lost hours are their own reward.

Since my own experience with camping in Europe is limited, I will refer you to books like *Two Wheel Travel*, edited by Peter Tobey and published by the Tobey Company, Box 428, New Canaan, Conn. 06840, and *Traveling By Bike*, available from World Publications, Box 366, Mt. View, Calif. 94040.

Hosteling started in Germany in 1910. A German school teacher named Richard Schirrmann saw the need for simple, inexpensive shelter for youthful travelers, whether by bicycle or on foot. These he called *Jugendherberge*, translated as youth hostels. The first hostels were indeed modest, being little more than the classrooms of school buildings that stood vacant during the summer. Later, when the idea spread, all sorts of buildings were converted into hotels so that today they can be anything from a cabin to a castle.

Today Europe has over 3000 hostels but they are not all of the same quality. The best hostel countries are north of the Alps. For a charge varying from $1–$2, you will find a cot in a dormitory, a reasonably clean bathroom, and usually a common room where you can sit, read and rest. Most hostels will also feed you, the charge varying from $1–$2 for dinner. A sleeping bag is not necessary. All you need is a sleeping sack, which you buy from any large hostel and take along with you. Blankets are supplied. (If you see the word *Fussende* on a blanket in a German hostel, that means literally foot-end or the end for your feet.) To use hostels, you have to be a member. For further information, write to American Youth Hostels, Delaplane, Va. 22025.

Having led several hostel trips, I am an enthusiast, but I will point out that hostels are not for everybody. Most American adults would be unhappy with the crowding and the lack of privacy. Another restriction is that you must be in by 10 p.m. Once I was taking a shower in the Salzburg hostel, when the lights went out. It was 10 p.m.!

There is no question in my mind that a hostel trip is the greatest educational experience in the world for a young person. We had arrived at the hostel at Spielmansau in Bavaria after a long, hard day on our bikes, and we were tired. At 10 p.m. we were fast asleep. At 11 p.m. the dormitory was invaded by a noisy group of German boys who had apparently come over the same roads we had. The only reason the house father let them in was that there wasn't another roof for miles around. Keyed up by their adventure, the German boys kept up a running dialogue that made it impossible to sleep. I told them to shut up in German and every other language I could think of. The only result was that the troublemakers now began to giggle and tussle. The situation was getting out of hand.

Our boys held a whispered conference. Faced with an invisible enemy in the pitchblack dorm, they had to rely on superior strategy. Getting up under cover of darkness, they rushed the German beds, grabbed their blankets, and threw them out the open window. Stunned, the German boys did not know what was happening until it was too late. Immediately there was a deathlike silence. We got ready for a counterattack, but it never came.

For the Germans, this raid meant a miserable night. Since the dorm was on the second floor and the outside door of a hostel is always locked at night, they could not retrieve the blankets. Temperatures that night fell to freezing. To top it off, the house father found the blankets the next morning and traced them to the Germans. Informed of what had happened, he gave them a severe dressing down. The Americans carried the day.

Another thing to remember about hostels is that they always stand on the highest mountain around. This nearly did us in at Todtnau. We got there in the late afternoon and went to the bakery to buy a birthday cake for Marilyn. The only cake available was a *Schwarzwaldkirschentorte* (Black Forest Cherry Torte), 18 inches in diameter. I bought it, thinking that the hostel was nearby. Cautiously riding my bike with the cake balanced on the handlebar, I was looking forward to the surprise party. Suddenly, the road left the valley and started climbing. I shifted into low, then low-low. The grade stiffened to 10 percent.

I got off and studied the map. Holy smokes. The hostel was at the 3500-foot level. Somebody observed ominously that Todtnauberg means mountain of death. We walked a mile. The road was now a boulder-strewn track. For four miles, we clawed our way up that vicious grade, with me balancing the bike in one hand and the cake in the other. Finally, after a two-hour struggle, we staggered up to the hostel just as dinner was being served. To this day, Marilyn cannot understand how that *Schwarzwaldkirschentorte* found its way to the mountain top.

I recommend hosteling for all young people with an itch to travel and the ability to cope.

We now come to hotels, the third travel-style, and I will include here also the private-home accommodations that are called bed-and-breakfast places in England and *pensions* on the Continent.

First, let me say that the small hotels of Europe, when they are not in big cities, are far more enjoyable, distinctive and restful than hotels in the Hilton class. True, the atmosphere is not always enchanting, but you nearly always find somebody who is fun to talk to. Nothing is more refreshing than to check into one of these small places, take a bath, put on clean clothes, and repair to the bar for a few drinks with the locals.

I will admit that countries vary widely. I once stayed in an English country-hotel, primarily for families. In the evening, although the lobby was full of people, nobody talked above a whisper. It was the most depressing place I have ever seen.

In contrast, in a *Bierstube* in St. Johann in Austria, I met a man who had been in the battle for Stalingrad and who was able to give me a vivid account of that epic struggle.

In Les Echarmeux in the French Midi, a mixed group of French and Americans sat at one big table. Among the Americans (all members of a bicycle-touring group) was an extremely attractive girl of Japanese extraction. Next to her was a local Frenchman, and on the other side of the Frenchman was Bob Ashby of Santa Ana. The Frenchman was so taken with the Japanese beauty that he could not refrain from putting his hand on her knee – under the table. Annoyed, Jeanne reported her predicament to Bob. After a whispered consultation, Bob and Jeanne changed places at a moment when the Frenchman was so busy arguing with the waiter that he did not notice.

Unaware of what had happened, the Frenchman filled his glass for the umteenth time, put his hand on what he thought was Jeanne's knee and squeezed. Slowly he came to the realization that it wasn't the same knee. Without bothering to find out who his new neighbor was, he finished his drink, slapped the table, and yelled, "Sabotage!"

An English pub, a French bistro, a German Bierstube all reflect the basic national attitudes. These attitudes surface much more quickly in the small town where people know each other than in the metropolis where people distrust each other. That is why the cycle tourist is at a tremendous advantage. He sees and meets the common people at their own level.

On tour with the International Bicycle Touring Society in France, Dr. Eugene Gaston and his wife, Helena, had become separated from the main group on account of tire trouble, which proved difficult to fix because they were riding an English tandem in a country with metric standards. The only one to witness the predicament was Fred DeLong, a respected authority on bicycling technology. After repeated but futile attempts to repair a broken casing on the tire, Fred decided that he would ride the 20 miles to Dijon while the Gastons made themselves comfortable in the nearby village. Fred was to return with a replacement tire as quickly as he could find one. He took off at two p.m. Meanwhile the Gastons pushed their tandem to the hamlet of Chambertin where Gene quickly spotted the village bistro. He carefully parked the tandem outside so that Fred would not overlook it. Then Gene and Helena went inside. They sat down and ordered a bottle of wine. Except for the patron, they were alone.

A short, stocky man in nondescript uniform entered the premises. He had seen the tandem and wanted to know if he could help. Gene did his best to explain, but there was the language barrier. Eventually Gene came to the conclusion that his newfound friend had a tandem at home and that it might be possible simply to exchange wheels. The proposal seemed to have little chance of success. Moreover, Gene was loath to do anything that might take him away from his post at the bistro. To sidetrack his would-be helper, Gene invited him inside for a glass of wine. The invitation was gladly accepted.

Obviously, an interpreter was needed. The patron and the newly arrived guest went into a huddle. Yes, they knew somebody in the village who could speak English. Although Gene never saw or heard a telephone, the bistro apparently had a very efficient communication system somewhere in the back. Before long a young man entered. As soon as he was apprised of the situation, he approached the Gastons.

"Do you speak English?" asked Gene.

"Oui, oui!"

Gene gave a minute description of the trouble that had overtaken him. He could have saved his breath. The interpreter's knowledge of English was limited to a few words so badly mispronounced they made no sense. At this impasse, Gene offered the man a glass of wine. Everybody sat down again. The party was getting cozy.

At this point, the local garage man appeared on the scene. He listened carefully, went outside to look at the tandem, took off, and eventually reappeared with a boot for the tire. It proved to be too small. He went for another boot. It was too large. Before he could go to any further trouble, Gene invited him inside for a glass of wine. The first bottle having been drained, Gene ordered another.

Gradually, other people entered. Whether they came for their regular aperitif or for a look at the stranded Americans, Gene never knew. What did it matter? Everybody was having a good time. The patron hauled out some more bottles. Gene toasted the French, and the French toasted the Americans. Each time a new guest entered, he was introduced to the Gastons and offered a drink. The small room now began to get crowded. The patron opened an adjoining room. Gene looked at his watch. It was getting on towards six p.m. Fred should be back any time.

Fred had not been idle, but his job was complicated by the size of Dijon and the tour group's sagwagon's absence on another mission. Eventually, however, he was able to find a replacement tire and to start on the return journey. Out of breath from his exertions, he spotted the tandem in the gathering darkness, parked his bike, and entered the bistro which by now was crammed with jabbering Frenchmen. So confused was the scene that Fred had trouble spotting the Gastons. Waving the precious tire overhead, he took a few steps, tripped over something on the floor, and landed flat on his face while the tire flew through the air and landed on the table of the Gastons. A tremendous cheer went up. The village had not seen such excitement in years.

The best reception I ever had was in Amsterdam. I had arrived at Schiphol airport late in the evening, ready to join a group from the International Bicycle Touring Society at a downtown hotel. Ordinarily, the ride from Schiphol to downtown is not difficult. But whether from the lateness of the hour, the new freeway, or the lack of an adequate map, I lost my way. After many wrong turns through deserted neighborhoods, I reached the hotel at 2 a.m. in the morning. Just looking at me, the room clerk knew that I was another huff-and-puffer. All day he had been checking them in. The singles and the couples, the fussy and the not-so-fussy, the easy-to-please and the hard-to-please. By this time, he had run out of private rooms and he wanted to dispose of me as quickly as he could.

"Ah, yes," he said, after asking me for my name. "I have you on the list." He spoke English very well but not well enough to know the colloquial meaning of what he said next.

"And who would you like to sleep with, sir?"

This situation nearly came to pass on another tour. We were traveling in France with a group of 20 Americans and a smaller number of French. Among the French was Sylviane Couve de Murville who was a niece of the then French foreign minister. Sylviane was a demure girl in her early twenties, a librarian brought up in the best French tradition. I think that this tour was her first experience with a large group of strangers. Partly because of her upbringing and partly because of the unusual circumstances, she was a picture of decorum.

In the small town of Egliseneuve d'Entraigues, we stayed in a rather drab hotel with four stories, all laid out in exactly the same way. One floor looked like every other. In America, you would still be able to tell the floor by the room number. But in France room numbers bear no predictable relationship to floors. So the stage was set for a mixup.

After a sumptuous dinner with too much wine, I suddenly felt very tired and a little dizzy. While the others repaired to the lounge, I excused myself, stepped into the elevator, and got off on the wrong floor. Walking to what I thought was my room, I found it unlocked and flopped in bed without even turning on the light. To tell you the truth, I was a little sick to my stomach. I must have fallen asleep immediately. In the middle of this wine-induced coma, I felt somebody tug at my arm.

"Doctor!" A female voice slowly penetrated my numbed senses. "What are you doing in my bed?" It was Sylviane.

So far I have talked about hotels. The alternative is the bed-and-breakfast place. They are common particularly in England and Germany. In England, they are listed in a directory published by the Cyclists Touring Club. In other countries, you may need a little help to find them. The best system is to go to the railroad station and ask for the traveler's aid. They have a list. In Germany, bed-and-breakfast places display a sign that says *Zimmer* or *Zimmer Frei. Zimmer* means room.

Prices vary according to the country. They are constantly going up, of course. In 1976 you should figure about $10 a day for food and overnight if you camp out or stay in hostels. This amount becomes $15 if you use bed-and-breakfast places, and $25 if you stay in hotels. These figures are based on travel in the country. In the larger cities, you should multiply them by two. England is the least expensive of the northern European countries, and Scandinavia the most expensive. France and Germany come in between.

Whether to go alone or in a group depends on your circumstances. I enjoy both. Alone, you make your friends as you go. In a group, you get lots of companionship but you cut yourself off from the natives. You can combine the two. Go with a group but do some freelancing before the group assembles or after it disbands.

The thing I like about freelancing is the challenge. The closest brush I ever had was in Norway. I was traveling in the fjord country, and I made the mistake of trying to get across a mountain range before dark. Dark comes late in Norway in the summer. Still, I was caught in the dense forests of the Jostedalsbreen without food or shelter when the light was gradually disappearing behind the bank of low clouds that promised snow. Just as the first flurries hit, I saw some log cabins in the woods. They looked deserted. However, as I drew closer, I saw a man by the side of the road. He was leaning against a tree, smoking a pipe and completely lost in thought. I think he was as surprised to see me as I was to see him. I don't speak Norwegian, but there is a universal language. We said hallo.

He motioned me to follow him. We walked about a quarter of a mile over a rutted track to the nearest cabin. I parked the bike while he lighted an oil lamp. That is when we first really saw each other. He was a heavyset man in his middle forties, a typical lumberjack. The cabin had a dozen doubledecker bunks and very little else. I figured that it was time to introduce myself.

"*Amerikaner.*" Most Norwegians speak a little German.

He answered right away, also in German. "You can sleep here." He pointed at one of the bunks. "Are you hungry?"

We walked to the next cabin, which was obviously a mess hall. He began to rummage through some cupboards and came up with a loaf of bread, a head of cheese, and two steaming cups of coffee. I gathered that he was the camp cook and caretaker. All the lumberjacks had gone to town since this was Saturday night. I tried to imagine the life of a logger at those latitudes, but I nearly fell asleep doing it. Olaf cleaned up, and I stumbled back to the dorm.

When I woke up the next morning, Olaf was standing over me with a mug of strong coffee. I looked around. All the bunks were occupied with snoring men. I dressed and made my way to the mess hall. It was nippy, and a thin layer of snow covered the ground.

Olaf busied himself at the stove. Although he had his back toward me and I couldn't see the stove, I could tell that he was making pancakes. He made them four at a time, throwing them high into the air and piling them neatly in a stack. All the while, he was either whistling or singing in a soft voice. I could tell that he was in high spirits.

When he was done, he divided the stack of cakes into two

The pleasantly winding lanes of Berkshire provide enjoyable cycling through the English countryside. Much of this land has remained unchanged for years and offers a glimpse into the peaceful past. (Bernard Thompson)

parts and brought them to the table. Apprehensively, I counted 12 cakes in each stack. Olaf went back for coffee. Then he sat down. His face was wreathed in smiles, and his eyes were sparkling. It was obvious that he had something on his mind.

"I have a sister in America," he said after his second mug. "But I have not heard from her in a long time. Maybe you know her."

"What is her name?"

"Sonja — Sonja Threlkjeld." He took a piece of paper and wrote the name in large letters. You could tell that he was better at handling an axe than a pen.

"She left when she was only 18," he said. "She was going to work for a family, a Norwegian family. She was to come back in a year. But then the war came."

"Where did the family live?"

Olaf tried to tell me, but I could not make it out. Finally he jumped up and went to a cupboard from which he pulled a worn and faded map of the United States. He put the map down with care.

"Here," he said, putting his finger on a spot that had been rubbed bare. I looked closely. It was Oconomowoc, Wisconsin.

"I am sorry," I said. "I have never been there."

A sudden change came over Olaf. His smile faded, his face

Cambo is a Northumbrian village of exceptional beauty. It is owned by the National Trust, an organization for the protection and preservation of the living environment. (Peter Knottley)

dropped, his shoulders sagged. It was obvious that he had pinned all his hopes on a positive answer. He pushed his plate away. I did too, but for a different reason. I offered to pay him, but he refused.

I packed my bags. The men in the dorm were still asleep. When I wheeled my bike toward the road, Olaf was standing in the same spot where he was the previous night. Again, he seemed to be in deep thought. I shook hands and thanked him. *"Auf wiedersehen."*

The snow was not deep enough to keep me from riding. At the next bend in the road, I looked back. Olaf was still standing there. As I rounded the bend, I took away his hope of finding his sister in America.

Whether you are traveling alone or with two or three, you have a better chance of such piquant encounters than in a group. You also have a better chance of meeting other cyclists. Still, you might spend all summer and not meet more than a handful. To see lots of them, you can go to the rallies. These rallies are well announced in the magazine of the Cyclists Touring Club. The annual rally in York usually comes the last weekend in June. Write to the CTC for details.

In France, the main rally is organized by the Federation Francaise de Cyclotourisme, 8 rue Jean-Marie Jego, Paris 75013. Date and place vary from year to year. Another interesting event in France that attracts thousands is Velocio Day. It is a hill-climb for people of all ages, held near St. Etienne, usually on the first weekend in July. Write to the Chambre Syndical du Cycle, 7 Karl Marx Boulevard, St. Etienne.

Finally, there is the rally of the cycling section of the Alliance Internationale de Tourisme. While not as large as the others, it is perhaps more interesting in that it is international. For information, write to the chairman, Mr. J. Przezdzieckie, Societe Polonaise de Tourisme, Senatorska 11, Warsaw 5, Poland. The address of the Alliance is 9 rue Pierre Fatio, Geneva, Switzerland.

How to Get Your Bike on Train or Plane

Most cyclists who are planning their first trip to Europe want to know whether they will have any trouble getting the bicycle aboard. Here is my own system.

I ride to the airport, park the bicycle in a safe place, and go to the check-in counter with the bags but not the bicycle. I then announce that I have a bicycle. On overseas flights, I have never had any trouble and I have never had to pay anything. Of course, my other baggage is very light, never more than 20 pounds, counting the bags. A friend, Ed Delano of Vacaville, Calif. tells me that he was not so lucky. He was charged $150 each way for extra baggage, which in his case consisted mainly of bicycle togs, parts and tools.

Domestic airlines solve the problem by selling you a plastic bag or carton for a few dollars. The plastic bag is the best. It accommodates the bicycle without the need to remove anything, and it is re-usable. A carton is much more awkward. If you want the plastic bag, go to American Airlines.

In all my experience as president of the International Bicycle Touring Society, I know of only one person who had trouble with his bike at the check-in counter on an international flight. Jerry Mason, of Kalamazoo, Mich., had flown to England on a Pan American flight, no questions asked. On the return flight, he tangled with a martinet at the counter. Never having handled a bicycle before, this man made a snap decision that the machine should be in a carton. Although Jerry patiently explained that there was no real need for this (the cargo hold of a jet has ample room), the man stood fast. Finally, Jerry moved to the TWA counter where he was very well received. Pan American later apologized for this incident.

There isn't any difficulty getting your bike on a train in Europe, either. Simply buy your ticket at the regular window. Then take your bike and ticket to the baggage department, which is usually some distance away. The attendant at the baggage counter will issue you a bicycle ticket and put it on the next train. The charge is a few dollars when you are on the Continent. In England, it is higher, one half of the passenger fare.

Occasionally your bicycle is delayed in transit, so I try to keep an eye on it. In England, I put the bike in the van myself. Elsewhere, this is not always possible. Delays come about chiefly when you cross an international border. If in doubt, reclaim the bike at the first major stop in the new country.

For the most part, the railroads do an excellent job. In Lyon, France I once had only five minutes between trains. Moreover, my new train was on a different platform. I held my breath. At the last moment, the baggage handler rushed up with my bike.

A friend was not so lucky. He had checked his bike through from Barcelona to Geneva. As the train left the Barcelona station, he saw his bike left behind on the platform. After a number of telephone calls and a wait of several days in Geneva, he gave up and continued by train. Six months later, he received a letter from the stationmaster in Barcelona. "We are holding your bike, and what do you want us to do with it?" This is the only instance I know of bike loss.

Your Baggage

This is not the place for a long dissertation on what to take. My best advice is that you have a dry run, so to speak, on a weekend well before your trip. By that, I mean go on a cruise with full pack. It is surprising how much you learn. You may be sorry if you don't.

On a tour of France, one of the participants arrived in Paris with a suitcase and a number of empty bicycle bags. On the morning of departure, he transferred the contents of the suitcase to the bags without having tested beforehand whether everything would fit. At the last moment he found that there was no room for his camera. Since time was now pressing, he simply fashioned a shoulder strap for the camera. However, he quickly discovered that the camera had a tendency to slide forward and hit his knee with every revolution of the cranks. To avoid the painful collisions, he now began riding bowlegged and he suffered severe knee strain before the first day was over. Although he corrected the problem on the second day, his knees gave him so much trouble that he had to go home early.

Taking too little can be almost as annoying. I remember a tour on which I forgot my belt. It took me half a day to find a shop where they could sell me another one. Buying everyday articles is very simple at home where you know all the shops for miles around. But in Paris or London it can be extremely frustrating.

When you start packing for your first trip, put all the articles on the table and weigh them individually. If the total weight is more than 15 pounds, you are taking too much. Start the elimination process, painful though it is. With drip-dry clothes, you need only two of everything. Take the smallest toothbrush, the smallest razor, the smallest cake of soap. Everything counts.

The only other bit of advice I have is the raincape. The bicyclist needs a raincape that is made for use on a bicycle. I have seen Americans in raintogs that are totally unsuitable. Ponchos are totally unsuitable, and so are raincoats. When in doubt, wait till you get to England. There, they know.

The Touring Bicycle

By the time you start on a tour of Europe, you should have learned enough to know what a touring bicycle is. It is not a 10-speed bicycle off the rack with fenders and carriers added as an afterthought. Fenders and carriers should be built into the frame at the time of manufacture. The basic differences between a touring bicycle and a bicycle that has been converted to a touring bicycle are these:

- A longer wheelbase and a greater fork rake for the

touring bicycle. These features make for comfort even though they detract from speed. Comfort is more important than speed.

● Wide-ratio gears with a bottom of 30 inches or even lower.

● Wired-on tires. I once met two American boys who were touring on sew-up tires. They had had a total of 15 flats. Since their tour was in a remote area, replacements were difficult and slow. When I asked them why they did not use wired-on tires, they said, "Never!" How ridiculous can you be?

● Built-in carriers. If you put a Pletscher carrier on the average bike, it sways under load. The carrier should be solidly fixed to the frame.

● Fenders. Once you have seen the mayhem that is visited on your fenderless bike in an all-day rain, you will agree. No self-respecting bicycle tourist in England or France ever rides without fenders. It simply does not make any sense.

One further word before I leave this subject. Unless you are an experienced mechanic, have your bike gone over carefully by an expert *before you leave.* On many occasions I have seen Americans arrive in Europe with bikes that were in need of a major overhaul. Spokes are particularly vulnerable when you put a load on your bike. Gear cables may be frayed, bottom brackets worn, free-wheels wilted, pedals creaky. Personally, I always install fresh cables and new tires before every European tour. Trying to do it on the road is a hassle.

For further information on this subject, I refer the reader to a book like Fred DeLong's *Bicycles & Bicycling*, available from World Publications, Box 366, Mt. View, Calif. 94040.

How to Get to Europe Cheap

The cheapest way to Europe is by charter flight. The trick is to get the exact dates you want. Even if you get the exact dates, you may run into unexpected delays.

My charter flight was to arrive in London on a Friday at 5 p.m. At 6 p.m. I was to meet a group of CTC members for the overnight ride to York where the rally was held that weekend. Unfortunately, my plane was held up in Toronto. Instead of arriving in London at 5 p.m., I arrived at 8 p.m. Too late to join the others, so I started by myself.

That was not so easy in the dark. Just getting out of London's airport was a job. I lost my way repeatedly. At 11 p.m., I sneaked into a pub in Luton just before it closed. Refreshed with a pork pie and a cup of tea, I re-entered the enveloping darkness.

At midnight it started to rain. I donned my cape, but now it became difficult to read the road signs. In addition, I was handicapped by not having good maps. By 3 a.m., I was famished again. No all-night restaurants in these little English villages. I had to push on, whether I wanted to or not.

At long last I came to what the English call a transport cafe. We would call it a truck stop. It was not very clean, but I sat down anyway. Knowing that breakfast is the one meal an English cook cannot foul up, I ordered it. The eggs were flawed, and the bacon was indigestible. I pushed on, as the rain increased. At 7 a.m. I looked out over the bleak landscape of The Wash. There must be an easier way of getting to York, I thought.

I finally got there on Saturday afternoon, after a 220-mile ride from London. That evening I fell asleep at the slide show. As soon as I got back to the hotel I went to my room and hit the sack. When I woke up, I figured it must be Sunday morning. But I could not be sure because my Accutron had given up the ghost. I dressed and went downstairs. "Where is breakfast," I asked.

The clerk looked at me in amazement. "Breakfast? That was over at 10 a.m.," he said.

"What time is it now?" I asked.

"Four o'clock!" Goodbye York Rally.

The lesson to be learned is that on a trip you must roll with the punches. Don't stick to plans when they become impractical. Make a new plan. Be flexible.

Exploring Europe

If you have your sights set on Germany, go to the Black Forest. The Moselle valley is also very lovely, but you can't see everything. It would be possible to go all the way from Holland to the Black Forest by boat, but the journey takes three days which is a big chunk of time.

The train covers the same route in eight hours. Get off the train at Baden-Baden, and you are at the northern edge of the Forest. Follow the suggestions offered earlier, and you will wind up on the Swiss border where you can regain your breath.

If, on the other hand, you have your sights set on France, take the train from Amsterdam to Paris. After a few days of sightseeing in that city, you should select *one* area for a leisurely tour. A good starting point is Brive, in south-central France. The train journey takes only four hours by *rapide*. These rapid trains do not have vans, however. Your bicycle will follow by slow freight and arrive a day later.

The country of Brive is open to you. No matter which way you go, you will be in ideal cycling country. The terrain varies from rolling to hilly, and that is something to be remembered in deciding on this or another area, and planning daily mileage. It is possible to get prepared itineraries from the French Federation for Cycletourism, but they are written in French and therefore of limited value to Americans.

There are two other possibilities in case Brive does not appeal to you. If you desire a tour in flat country, go to the

It is no shame to walk up a grade like this one in Ireland. It takes about two hours to walk and wheel your bicycle up Connor Pass, and about 10 minutes to coast down, provided no sheep get in your way. The surrounding countryside appears desolate for miles around. (D. Colligan)

Loire valley and visit the castles. For the chateau country, take the train to Tours and start there.

If the mountains appeal to you, try the Vosges, the Alps and the Pyrenees. For the Vosges, take the train to Strasbourg and begin there. A trek to the Alps should begin in either Geneva or Nice. Start in Perpignan for a trip to the Pyrenees.

It doesn't matter whether you choose France or Germany, you will find yourself on or near the Swiss border in three weeks. Switzerland is a country better viewed by train if it is the last week of your vacation and you are uncertain about tackling a lot of climbing. You are now in Europe's heartland. Austria, Bavaria and Italy are within easy reach. Make your way back to pick up your bike, or you can forward it to Paris or your departure point. Always allow a few extra days if the unaccompanied bike has to cross international borders.

Reference Sources

Whether your primary interest is people, scenery, history or architecture, the bicycle will lead you to it better than anything else. The bicycle traveler has the priceless advantage of doing the thing at his own pace. No other method of travel has this degree of freedom.

Bicycle Touring in Europe, by Karen and Gary Hawkins, is a 184-page paperback, published in 1973 by Random House. It brings together most of the basic information in highly readable form. The Hawkins book is the informal style and features personal insights. The writers show how they were able to penetrate the veneer by melting into the population.

In addition, the book is encyclopedic in listing everything that touches on the life of the bicycle tourist. The only

The remains of Bythorn Abbey in Yorkshire are still impressive. England is one of the best countries for bicycle touring. The countryside is beautiful, the roads relatively flat, and the people speak your language. (Bernard Thompson)

weakness might be insufficient attention to the important matter of avoiding traffic.

The companion volume for the English reader has just been published. It is called *Cycle Touring in Europe*, by Peter Knottley, published by Constable of London. A 250-page $6 hardback, it covers much the same ground as the Hawkins book.

Again, the book is encyclopedic in nature. It takes up each country in turn and tells you how to get there, where to go, what to see, and even covers expenses.

A third book of interest is the *Youth Hosteler's Guide to Europe,* staff-written by the Youth Hostels Association in England. The American edition was published in 1973, virtually unchanged. It is a 492-page paperback that sells for $2.95. The book covers 22 countries in more detail than the other two books. It has many sketch maps and outlines a number of tours in each country.

Most youth hostel associations in Europe concern themselves more with the running of hostels than with the promotion of bicycle travel. Once the hostel associations reached their present size, they were forced to attract ever *more* business. When the supply of bicyclists was insufficient to fill the hostels, the associations had to accept non-hostelers, mainly hitchhikers and bus travelers. In none of the European countries are the bicyclists represented by the hostel associations. The bicyclists have their own associations.

Addresses of Organizations

American Youth Hostels, Delaplane, Virginia 22025

League of American Wheelmen, 19 South Bothwell, Palatine, IL 60067

International Bicycle Touring Society, 846 Prospect, La Jolla, CA 92037

Cyclists Touring Club, 69 Meadrow, Godalming, Surrey, England

Federation Francaise de Cyclotourisme, 8 rue Jean-Marie Jego, Paris 75013

Dutch Touring Club, 5 Museum Plein, Amsterdam, The Netherlands

Suggested Itineraries

Of the six detailed itineraries that follow, three are easy, two are moderately difficult, and one is recommended for strong riders. Easy tours are through England, Holland and the Loire valley. More difficult trips are the Black Forest and the Vosges. The tour of the Pyrenees requires the ability to climb and rough it.

The suggested overnight stops are about 50 miles apart. On tour, you spend much time finding your way, looking around, talking to people, etc. It is better to have a little time left over than not enough.

In popular districts, particularly the Black Forest, it is advised to call ahead for reservations. If you are hosteling, you need the hostel directory from American Youth Hostels, Delaplane, Virginia 22025.

England. Use Barts (short for Bartholomews) maps 14, 19, 7, 8, 5 and 9, old series (1 to 126,720). Start in Oxford, finish in London.

First day. Map 14. Northwest on A-34 to Woodstock. A mile beyond the town, switch to yellow road to Charlbury. Then Chipping Norton, Moreton on the Marsh, Stretton on the Foss, Ilmington (shift to map 19) and Stratford. Overnight.

Second day. South to Broadway through Chipping Campden. Back to map 14. Straight south on yellow road to Snowshill. Then Ford and Kineton. Then west to Cheltenham through Charlton Abbots. Overnight.

Third day. South six miles on A-435 to Cockleford. Then Elkstone, Winstone, Sapperton and Malmesbury. Map 7. Southwest to Foxley, Norton, Hullavington and Castle Combe. To Bath for overnight.

Fourth day. Southeast to Bradford, Trowbridge and Edington. Then over the Salisbury Plain to Tilshead. Map 8. Maddington, Rollestone and Stonehenge, an impressive display of prehistoric monoliths. South to Salisbury for overnight.

Fifth day. Map 5. East six miles to the Grimsteads. Then continuing east, to West Dean, Dunbridge Station, Michelmarsh, Braishfield, Standon and Winchester. Overnight.

Sixth day. East on A-31 to Ropley Dean. Then on yellow road to Ropley and East Tilstead. Map 9. Continue east to Selborne and Oakhanger Ponds. North to Kinsley. Northeast by east through Elstead to Godalming and Guildford for overnight. Train to London.

Holland. This is a circle tour, beginning and ending in Amsterdam. Get your maps first (order from Dutch Touring Club, address in previous section). You need four sheets: North Holland, South Holland, the Veluwe, and Utrecht. Bicycle paths appear on these maps as a single red line with cross hatches. The Dutch Touring Club has erected numerous road markers and they are all numbered. This same number appears on your map. Orientation is therefore easy.

First day. Amsterdam to Leiden. Find the Amstel River on your map. It is in the southern part of the city. The street alongside the river is the Amsteldijk (dike of the Amstel). It takes you to Ouderkerk and Uithoorn, about 10 miles. Continue west through Vrouwenakker, Bilderdam and Leimuiden. From here south to Soubrugge, then west to Hoogmade and Leiden. Overnight.

Second day. Leiden to Alkmaar. Head for the coast at Katwijk and follow the bicycle path north. You are in the dunes, at arm's length from the sea. Continue through the Kennemer Dunes to Velsen. Across the North Sea Canal by ferry. Then again through the dunes to Egmond. Here, turn inland for Alkmaar. This town is famous for the cheese market every Friday.

Third day. Alkmaar to Kampen. East to Schermerhoorn

and Evenhoorn. Then Hoorn. Now over the dike through Oosterleek to Enkhuizen where you pick up a boat for Urk. Urk is a fishing village which does not welcome visitors on Sunday. From Urk you head east over reclaimed land until you get to Kampen. Use map of the Veluwe.

Fourth day. Kampen to Apeldoorn. These cities are only 25 miles apart, leaving you plenty of time to zigzag on the terrain to the west, the Veluwe. It is a sparsely settled tract with lots of heather and lots of bicycle paths, away from roads. Swing through villages like Nunspeet, Vierhuizen and Elspeet. Overnight in Apeldoorn, a summer resort with many fine hotels.

Fifth day. Apeldoorn to Doorn. Continue your exploration of the Veluwe in a westerly direction. Don't miss the van Gogh museum at Hoenderloo. Head east through Otterloo, Lunteren and Renswoude. Many hotels in Doorn.

Sixth day. Doorn to Amsterdam. Pick your way through towns like Den Dolder, Lage Vuursche, Nieuw Loosdrecht, Our Loosdrecht, Loenen and along the Vecht to Amsterdam. On your six-day ride, you will never be over 100 feet above sea level.

Germany. The Black Forest stretches along the east bank of the Rhine between Basel and Karlsruhe. Barely 100 miles north-south and 50 miles east-west, it makes up in beauty what it lacks in size.

The Black Forest is also famous for its spacious valleys, picturesque villages, and extensive hiking trails. These trails are well marked.

If you are using the Shell maps, get sheets 21 and 24.

Meeting the ordinary people who live in the countries you visit is easy to accomplish when you adapt yourself to the local customs. Visiting an English pub or inn can be one of the greatest pleasures of your tour. The "Hark to Bountry" is a typical English inn set in Lancashire's Trough of Bowland country. It is in the attractive village of Slaidburn. (Bernard Thomspon)

Sometimes these are printed on both sides. Try to stay on the yellow roads. All travel in the Black Forest is either up or down. There is very little flat ground.

First day. Baden-Baden to Wildbad. Soon after leaving Baden-Baden in an easterly direction on a red road, pick up the yellow to Forbach. Then north on the red road to Hilpertsau. Then east again on the yellow to Reichental and Christophshof. Then north to Wildbad.

Second day. Wildbad to Freudenstadt. Go south one mile on the red road to Ziegelhutte where you pick up a tiny yellow road that takes you to Aichelberg and the red road just beyond. From here you can get to Freudenstadt, either over the red road or through the country to the east with villages like Eisenbach and Hochdorf.

Third day. Freudenstadt to Triberg. Heading southwest, you pick up the yellow road to Wolfach as soon as you leave Freudenstadt. Then by red road to Gutach and by yellow road to Triberg. A variation would be to go over Schomberg to Schiltach, then to Schramberg, then to Gutach. The climbs are severe, but the views are superb.

Fourth day. Triberg to Titisee. Your road leads through Furtwangen. South of here, you have a choice. You can go through the valley at Urach and Eisenbach or through Erlenbach and Hinterzarten. Titisee is a big resort. You can sail and swim there.

Fifth, sixth and seventh day. You can easily spend three days going from Titisee in one of three directions: southwest to Basel, straight south to the Rhine, or southeast to Schaffhausen. This whole area is known for its deep, winding gorges. Seven miles west of Titisee is the Feldberg, highest point in the forest.

France. First, take a five-day tour of the Vosges mountains which stretch along the west bank of the Rhine opposite the Black Forest. Michelin map 62. Main roads are marked N (for national). Secondary roads are marked D (for *departmentale*). Local roads are marked VO or VV (for *voie ordinaire* or *voie vicinale*). Try to stay on the secondary roads. The tour outlined here is entirely in the mountains. You can also spend a few days combing the wine villages facing the Rhine.

First day. Epinal to Gerardmer. Epinal is 65 miles southwest of Strasbourg. Leaving Epinal, head southeast on D-42 to Jarmenil, then northeast on N-59 to Docelles, then southeast on D-11 to Le Tholy, then south on unnumbered road to Manaurupt. Continue on same road over the Sapois pass to Gerardmer. Overnight.

Second day. Northeast on D-23 to Le Rudlin. Then on unnumbered road over the Luschpach pass to Lac Blanc. Now south on D-48 over the Wettstein pass and then straight east on D-11 to Colmar. Overnight.

Third day. North through Ingerheim, Bennwhire, Riquewihr, to Ribeauville. Continue north through Thannenkirch and Haute Koenigsbourg to Selestat. From here, north over many little roads to Andlau. Then west on N-425 to Hohwalk. When you run out of steam, pick an overnight spot.

Fourth day. Southwest in the general direction of St. Die. Eventually you pick up D-214 to Ranrupt. Then east on N-424 to Ville. Finally west again on D-39 and D-23 to Provencheres. Overnight in St. Die.

Fifth day. Southwest on N-420 to Brouvelieurcs, then Bruyeres, then along the Vologne to Docelle and Jarmenil. Back to Epinal the same way you started.

A second tour in France is through the Loire valley, famous for its castles. This is rolling country without severe climbs. The chateaus stretch for about 100 miles, mainly south of the Loire. The best part is between Tours and Blois. Michelin map 64. Try to pick up a Michelin guidebook in English.

Start in Tours. Move west along the north bank of the Cher on D-288. Cross to the south bank at Savonnieres and continue to Villandry. Then on to Langeais, a few miles downstream. Follow D-16 along the south bank of the Loire till you come to Usse. From Usse you make a U-turn and go east on

D-7, then D-17 to Azay-le-Rideau. You can stay overnight here.

Continue along the north bank of the Indre to Montbazon. From here, on green-bordered D-17, to Truyes and La Bruyere. Cross the river and pick up D-10 to San Quentin, then D-80 to Chenonceaux. Travel on D-17 to Pouille, then Cour-Cheverny which is 16 miles to the north. Then on to Chambord. Remain overnight in Blois, which features a richly ornamental castle.

Spain. The tour outlined takes in the south face of the Pyrenees. This is remote and isolated country. Far from civilization, you must be prepared to find your own way and make your own repairs in case of mechanical trouble. You will be in mountains rising over 6,000 feet and will see villages that are rarely visited by tourists. Michelin maps 42 and 43, scale 1 to 400,000. Also map 86, scale 1 to 200,000.

Take the overnight train from Paris to Biarritz in the extreme southwest corner of France. On your bike, go southeast a few miles until you come to the village of Negresse near the airport. Pick up D-254, leading straight east a few miles until you pick up D-3, moving south to St. Pee. Three miles south of St. Pee, D-3 becomes D-4.

Actually, D-4 is two roads. One leads to Sare, the other to Dancharia. Take the one to Sare and ask if you can cross the border on D-306 to Echalar. If so, continue a few miles beyond Echalar to C-133 and turn south till you come to Santesteban, which is ideal for a good overnight. If you cannot get across on D-306, you will have to cross at Dancharia and go south on N-121 till you come to Santesteban.

The next day, retrace your tracks a few miles to Mugare and head south to Olague where you pick up an unnumbered

A long, straight, flat road ahead of you promises another day of pleasurable touring. This one is typical of Ireland. (D. Colligan)

road straight east to Zubiri. From here you make for Burguete on C-135.

The following day, retrace your tracks a few miles and pick up an unnumbered road leading southeast through Garralde, arriving in Garayoa and Jaurrieta where there is a good hotel. You can go on to Escaroz and take your chance on the hotel there. After Escaroz, follow the river north to Ochagavia, and across the pass to Isaba. From here travel north a few miles till you see the road to Zuriza, then south to Anso.

From Anso, follow the valley south. Travel east on N-240 to Puente la Reina where you pick up C-134 to Jaca.

Next day travel north to Biescas, then east to Torla. Spend the following day in the Park of the Ordesa, six miles to the north. From Torla, move south to Boltana and Ainsa. Take C-140 to Arro and Fuendecamp, then Campo. Take C-139 to Castejon.

The following day, go east on C-144 to N-230, turning north for Viella. A little before Viella, you pass through a three-mile tunnel, fortunately downhill. Shift to map 86 and go east from Viella on C-142 to Llavorsi and Sort for your overnight. Shift to map 43.

Next day, head due east from Sort over tracks and trails through villages such as Vilamur, les Lacunes, Guils and Pallerolls. Finish your tour by heading for Andorra and Aix-les-Thermes in France.